D1260628

Modern Hebrew

MODERN HEBREW

by

ELIEZER RIEGER

PHILOSOPHICAL LIBRARY
NEW YORK

Printed in the United States of America

 200

TABLE OF CONTENTS

INTRODUCTION

The principal aim of the following pages is to reduce the gap between the progress of research in the teaching of a second language, and current practice in the teaching of Hebrew. While much headway was made in the scientific treatment of foreign language teaching in the period between the two wars and especially since the Second World War, the teaching of Hebrew has benefited little from it, and most Hebrew textbooks and teachers—even gifted teachers—select conventional subject matter and adopt primitive teaching methods. The result is that the study of Hebrew by most students outside Israel leads only too often to failure and frustration. Even in Israel, where the knowledge of Hebrew has become a vital necessity and the influence of a Hebrew-speaking population naturally helps new immigrants to acquire the language, the rate of achievement has been far too slow.

This book is intended to serve as a guide for Hebrew teachers, curriculum planners and compilers of textbooks in the methods of imparting an elementary knowledge of Hebrew as a second language. I have no doubt that, through a sound application of modern linguistic science and pedagogy, it will be possible to register better achievements than hitherto in the teaching of Hebrew as a second language for those who study it outside Israel, and to shorten considerably the period of adaptation required by the masses of immigrants in Israel.

In preparing my investigations into the vocabulary, grammar, pronunciation and teaching methods of Hebrew I was guided by similar research in other languages, especially in English. The specific problems of Hebrew, which is so different from European languages, do not obscure the fact that there exists a common stock of pedagogic concepts on ways and means of teaching a foreign language. For this reason I dare to hope that my observations on the teaching of Hebrew as a second language, and my conclusions, which are incorporated in the "Jerusalem Method," may make some contribution to the search for new and effective approaches to second language teaching in general.

This book is the result of work done at the School of Education of the Hebrew University in Jerusalem. Through its encouragement and help this work has been made possible. For years I had the advantage of conducting a seminar with students who discussed with me several of the problems expounded here, and they also assisted me in assembling experimental material. My friends and colleagues, Professors Alexander M. Dushkin and Leon Roth of the Hebrew University, took the trouble to read my manuscript and gave me their critical observations.

Valuable help was rendered by Dr. Ralph Weiman of Philadelphia, who took an active part in the intensive language studies with the U. S. Army Specialized Training Program (A.S.T.P.). It was he who urged me to publish this book in English, guided me with his advice and even took on himself to translate it and read the proofs. My friends, Professor Abraham I. Katsh of New York University, Dr. Azriel Eisenberg, Executive Vice-President of the Jewish Education Committee of New York, and Dr. Judah Pilch, Executive Director of the American Association for Jewish Education, collaborated with me and encouraged me to publish this book, and Dr. Katsh was also kind enough to read the proofs.

In carrying out the plans for publication I was assisted by the American Friends of the Hebrew University, and especially by its Executive Director, Mr. Harry Friedgut. Through their good offices Mrs. Harold E. Beckman, of White Plains, N. Y., transmitted her generous gift which was instrumental in expediting the production of the book.

If this book helps to render the Hebrew language more widely known and spoken, that will be a fitting reward for all those who helped me and cooperated with me, both those whom I have mentioned by name and those whom I have not mentioned.

Hebrew University, Jerusalem

May, 1952

CHAPTER ONE

HEBREW AS A SECOND LANGUAGE FOR JEWS IN THE DIASPORA

The Reasons for Our Lack of Success in Language Teaching.

In practically every country we hear from time to time criticisms of scholastic attainments—the students do not know enough arithmetic, history, geography, science, etc. Yet in no subject has the lack of success been more glaring than in the teaching of foreign languages. In other subjects something at least is accomplished; moreover it is difficult to determine the extent of our failure since there are no generally accepted yardsticks by which our achievement can be measured. Educators claim that even if they do not succeed in imparting a great deal of specific information, they are at least helping in the formation of the student's character, in the development of his powers of reasoning, his taste, etc.—all very important educational ends.

The situation is however less vague with regard to the teaching of foreign languages. Here our failure is obvious to everyone. After years of study students cannot read, write or speak a foreign language. Nor are there, as in the case of other subjects, any substantial "associate or concomitant learnings." Most of the time spent on foreign language study is drudgery, and an appalling waste of time and effort at that. There is general agreement that "not one pupil in a hundred learns to speak and understand or even to read a foreign language." [1]

This seems to be the situation in the Hebrew schools in the Diaspora. The number of students who learn to read and write is extremely small. A large number drop out after a short period of time and those who remain usually lose their initial drive. Under such circumstances teachers are understandably disheartened.

The lack of success in teaching foreign languages in general and Hebrew in particular is due to several causes. We shall here indicate two of the more general ones:

1. There is a lack of a clearly defined goal. Most teachers and students have no clear idea of their objectives in teaching or studying a foreign language. Good intentions do not suffice—one must know exactly what one wants to achieve and direct his efforts towards the achieving of that particular goal. There must also be clearly defined stages so that the student can check his progress and know that he is indeed on the way to attaining his objective. We have, for example, no clear conception of our objectives in teaching Hebrew in the Diaspora and consequently no way of determining whether our students are making satisfactory progress or not.

2. Our classroom practice does not reflect the latest achievements in language pedagogy. Comparatively little use is made in the classroom of the important research work which has been done in the field of language instruction or of linguistic science. There is comparatively little application of recent work in language methodology (direct or natural method, motivation, functional and corrective grammar, modified forms of the translation method, phonetic instruction, audio-visual aids, frequency lists and lists of basic words, related and meaningful material, etc.). The achievements in all these fields amount to a silent revolution in language teaching but they are without value until they are applied in our day-to-day language teaching. Their use would not make language learning easier—learning a language will always require considerable effort—but would certainly make it more efficient.

We shall discuss in the following pages what we consider to be the most important objectives in the teaching of Hebrew. We shall not enter into a detailed analysis of the available curricula and our own current teaching methods since this would require more space than we have at our disposal here.[2]

Our Goals in Language Teaching

In any learning process it is essential that our objectives be clearly defined. If we know exactly what we want to achieve we can work out efficient techniques. If our goals are not clear we cannot work out an effective program of study nor measure the progress of our work.

Determining our goals in language instruction is basically a sociological problem. Language is a social institution and serves the purpose of society. It is therefore far from simple to determine what our goals should be in language teaching.

The statistical method cannot help us in this problem; for

statistics may help in fact-finding but not in setting goals. To be sure, it has been used for want of anything better. If we were, for example, to ask the Hebrew teachers and students in the Diaspora what purpose they had in teaching or studying Hebrew and then sort out their answers, we would have statistical material about our problem, but not necessarily a solution. We would know how many times certain answers were given, but the answers might not be good ones. A "scientific approach" of this sort may help to give status to unsound objectives and perpetuate existing prejudices and procedures which have grown up over the years. The curriculum makers who based their objectives on statistical studies of this sort caused more harm than good. They considered the problem "scientifically" solved when in reality "the underlying questions in education cannot by any dexterity of manipulation be converted into questions of science." [3]

We must therefore recognize that our problem cannot be solved with mathematical certainty. On the other hand we cannot afford to base our educational objectives on intuition or hunches. We have to base our conclusions on careful observation and analysis of all available data and on the considered judgment of specialists in the field. If we do so, we find that objectives in teaching foreign languages in general and Hebrew in particular fall into three categories:

1. Practical Objectives
2. Cultural Objectives
3. Emotional Objectives

Practical Objectives

There are important practical reasons for studying Hebrew today. The establishment of the State of Israel which has made Hebrew the official language of a government and its institutions has increased the practical importance of Hebrew. A knowledge of Hebrew is important for visitors to Israel and particularly so for prospective immigrants, and for those in the Diaspora who want to keep in close touch with life in Israel.

For Jews living in the Diaspora Hebrew is also important for conducting business with Israel or with Jews in other countries. There is a need for Hebrew teachers and for workers in Zionist and other bureaus. The tourist who wants to derive full benefit from his visit to Israel should be able to converse with the Israelis he meets, read the newspapers, listen to radio broad-

casts, attend meetings, visit the theater, etc. Even a knowledge
of the mere rudiments of Hebrew, the so-called "first-aid expressions," will add immeasurably to his visit.

And yet all these practical considerations are not in themselves sufficient to impel Jews in the Diaspora to undertake the
difficult task of learning Hebrew.

Cultural Objectives

The cultural value of foreign language study has several
aspects. The best way to understand one's own language is to
study a second language. A completely monolingual nation
does not have a highly developed linguistic sense. Just as we
can develop our own personalities only through contact with
others, so we cannot completely understand our own language
until we are able to compare it with others. In fact we can
best gain an appreciation of the particular genius of our own
language by comparing it with languages which are very different in structure. Many educators have considered the study of
Latin important for this very reason. Since Hebrew belongs to
another language family, speakers of Indo-European languages
may sometimes find the study of Hebrew more rewarding than
the study of Latin.

The study of a second language opens up wide horizons. A
monolingual people cannot help being provincial in its outlook.
The classical Roman educational system in the past had a
bilingual basis, as has the Swiss educational system today. The
study of the classical languages, particularly Latin, fulfilled a
similar function for many generations. The study of foreign
languages creates a common ground between nations and provides a vehicle for cooperation and sympathetic insight. It
helps to bring us closer to the ideal of "One World."

These considerations apply to the study of any language
which is the bearer of an important culture, but they apply with
particular force to the study of Hebrew. It is appropriate that
non-Jews as well as Jews should study Hebrew, since it is the
language of the Bible. During the Renaissance and the following period Hebrew was studied in the schools as one of the
classical languages. It was also studied in the early American
colleges. During the seventeenth century Hebrew was considered the mother of European languages. No student
could complete college without a knowledge of Hebrew. The
commencement addresses were on Hebrew themes. Indeed

during the American Revolution it was even proposed that Hebrew be made the official language of the nation.[4]

Hebrew has a special importance for the Jews in the Diaspora. It is not a "foreign language" for them. It is a language which binds them to their people's past and to their historic home as well as to their people in present-day Israel. It is also the language of their religion, the language of the Bible and the Prayerbook. It is the common denominator of all Jewish groups wherever they may live and whatever their particular characteristics.

Hebrew is the only language which is at once classical and modern. The difference between the Hebrew of the Bible and modern Hebrew is very small compared with the difference between classical and modern Greek or between Sanskrit and Hindustani. Israeli school children, for example, have no difficulty in understanding passages read to them from the Bible. In fact they often find biblical Hebrew easier than many modern Hebrew poems and literary productions.

Hebrew can also serve as an "international" language, uniting World Jewry in various parts of the globe. It is natural therefore that Hebrew should be taught as a second language in Jewish schools throughout the Diaspora. In America we have the phenomenon of Yiddish newspapers with an "English page" —the Yiddish part of the paper expressing the tie with the past and the English part reflecting the life centered on the present. Perhaps in the future we may witness a Hebrew page in the Anglo-American press—the Hebrew section reflecting not only the tie with the past but also interest in present-day Israel and its culture.

Emotional Objectives

Jews in the Diaspora do not study Hebrew solely because of the practical and cultural considerations we have just described. Some writers have indeed questioned whether the practical objectives can really justify the time and effort spent on studying foreign languages.[5] Nor are cultural considerations in themselves sufficient; one might argue that except for the most advanced students, it is easier to gain an insight into a foreign culture through translations than through reading foreign texts.[6] It is true, as some have argued, that a knowledge of Hebrew enables the Jew to understand the prayers of his people; but even here one can grasp the content more easily through translation.

Even more significant than the practical and cultural considerations for the study of Hebrew is the emotional one. The destruction of European Jewry and the rise of the Jewish State have led, among other things, to a desire to study Hebrew and to learn more about Hebrew culture. Speaking and reading Hebrew serves as a means of identifying oneself more closely with the Jewish nation. Language plays a most important role in social identification. It has served as a touchstone for distinguishing friend from enemy. The Greeks called other nations "barbarians," from the Greek word for "babbling," and the Slavic peoples called other nations "speechless" or "dumb."

There is no more powerful factor in creating group unity than a common language. One can best come to know another people through its language. In the case of Hebrew one can best identify himself with the Hebrew nation in the past and present through learning and using Hebrew.

Though the Jewish people has used many languages, only whatever was created in Hebrew has lasted. Works like *Emunot Vedeot* or *More Nebuchim* which were originally written in Arabic have been preserved as standard works of Jewish thought only because they were translated into Hebrew. Jewish studies and ideas expressed in other languages never exercised an enduring influence as have those written in Hebrew. As Bialik has put it,[7] "Language is the soil for the spiritual life of a nation. Just as all natural wealth comes from the earth and returns to the earth, so spiritual wealth comes from language and returns to language. Systems are born and pass away— their residues survive in language."

Should the Various Language Skills Be Taught Simultaneously or in Succession?

We have discussed so far the practical, cultural and emotional objectives in studying a language. We can now consider how these objectives may be achieved.

For language teaching to succeed there must be a series of stages leading to the ultimate goal. If we consider the processes involved in language learning, we find that we can distinguish between two passive ones—hearing and reading, and two active ones—speaking and writing. Hearing and speaking are, of course, closely related in that both involve the sounds of the language; reading and writing, on the other hand, deal with graphic symbols representing the sounds of the language.

In the historical development of language and in the lin-

guistic development of the child these four processes develop
in the following order: understanding the spoken language,
speech, reading, and writing. Is it better to teach all four skills
at once, or one after the other (or at least in three stages, since
understanding the spoken language and speaking are closely
related)? The question is far from academic: the answer we
give determines the measure of success we are likely to achieve.
The earlier opinion was that it was better to deal with all four
processes at once rather than to concentrate on any particular
one.[8] However, language teachers in the last generation have
come to recognize that we have to concentrate on one process
at a time (treating the understanding of the spoken language
and speaking as one process). We ordinarily have so little
time at our disposal that it is impossible to achieve anything
substantial if we try to teach all four skills;[9] moreover, we run
the risk that our students will become frustrated by their lack
of achievement and consider their language study a mistaken
investment.

If the student can devote ample time to language study we
ought, of course, to take up speaking, reading and writing. There
will be a certain degree of transfer from one skill to another if we
carefully direct our teaching to this end: the better the student
learns to speak the better he will read, and the better he reads
the better he will write. But we must face the fact that in most
cases there is not sufficient time for us to be able to do justice
to all four skills, and that it is better to concentrate on one skill
—or the related skills of understanding the spoken language and
speaking—so that the students may develop a certain proficiency
in at least one. If most of our students study a foreign
language for several years without feeling that they have learned
anything, the main reason is that we try to teach four different
skills in a period of time scarcely sufficient for developing proficiency in even a single one. Such an ambitious goal makes
"failure inevitable."[10]

A simultaneous frontal attack on the four skills should be
avoided. In most cases, it is the royal road to failure. If the
time at our disposal is too limited to teach all four skills we would
do better to teach one skill at a time: first, understanding and
speaking, then reading, and finally writing. If the Jewish
student in the United States, South Africa, France or Persia will
learn to speak a little Hebrew, perhaps he will have an incentive
to continue his studies and learn to read and even write it. As

it is, our students become discouraged after a year or two and drop the study of Hebrew with a feeling that they have learned little if anything. No attempt is made to teach them to speak. They are not able to read Hebrew (except for the few passages they learned in class) and they certainly cannot write it. However, if they feel that they have achieved some degree of proficiency in at least one skill they are likely to want to go on and to acquire the other skills as well.

If the readers wonders at this point what degree of proficiency we have in mind when we talk about learning to speak, read or write, we may say that we mean a degree sufficient to enable a student to exercise these skills almost automatically, that is, to be able to concentrate on the meaning rather than on details of vocabulary and grammar. If a student can express thoughts in sentences without having to think about each word and grammatical form, we can say that he has acquired a speaking knowledge of the language. The same thing is true of reading. If he can read a simple text and concentrate on the meaning without worrying about the individual words and grammatical forms, then he has a reading knowledge. If he can write a Hebrew letter and concentrate on what he wants to say rather than on the individual words and phrases, then he has a writing knowledge of Hebrew.

How Long Does It Take to Learn Hebrew?

The author asked many teachers how long they thought it took to teach an average high school student or adult in a class of 15 to 20 students to understand and speak, read and write Hebrew, using the definition just given. Most of the teachers were surprised at the question and explained that they had never considered the problem in terms of time or as a fourfold approach to language processes. They were then asked what answer they would give to a prospective student who wanted to know how many hours or how many months he would have to spend in order to achieve one or all of the above mentioned objectives. Some said 25 hours and some 1,000. (It was assumed that the number of hours given would include hours spent on homework as well as in the classrooms.)

Only a few gave figures which more or less tallied or which corresponded to the figures given during the last war by American and British experts in connection with the teaching of English. In the instructions given in the books issued by the

U. S. Army Language Section it was stated that experience has shown that it is possible through the use of suitable methods to teach students to speak a language fluently in from 6 to 9 months, devoting 15 hours a week to it.[11] In a report given by the Undersecretary of Foreign Affairs in the British Parliament (March 20, 1946), it was stated that it had proved possible to teach European languages, including the Balkan languages, in 6 to 9 months. Students were able after this time to speak fairly fluently and had made considerable progress in reading.[12]

The problem has not as yet been investigated satisfactorily for the study of Hebrew, but on the basis of the opinion of experienced teachers and the research work done in other countries we can venture the following figures: it takes from 200 to 250 hours to teach a student both to understand and to speak Hebrew, 800 to 900 hours to teach him to speak and read, and 1800 to 2000 to teach him to speak, read and write. These figures apply to average high school and adult students studying in classes from 15 to 20 under the guidance of experienced teachers. Children learn to speak a foreign language more rapidly but are slower in learning to read and write.[13] It is obvious that students studying in smaller classes, or receiving private instruction, will make more rapid progress. It should also be pointed out that the figures refer to students studying Hebrew abroad where they do not hear it spoken around them. Immigrants in Israel studying Hebrew, or youngsters studying Hebrew in summer camps where Hebrew is spoken, will naturally make more rapid progress in learning to speak.

Recent experience in foreign language teaching has compelled language experts to revise their ideas about the optimal distribution of instructional periods. It used to be held that if the students were asked to spend too many hours a week studying a foreign language, they would lose patience. Accordingly, schools devoted only from three to five hours a week to foreign language study. During the last war and immediately afterwards, a number of important experiments were conducted in which students studied the language from 3 to 5 hours a day and in some cases even longer. The results showed that the earlier belief had no foundation. If we interest our students properly and if they feel that they are rapidly acquiring the ability to speak and read a foreign language, we can increase the number of hours of language instruction very considerably. Language experts are now inclined to believe that devoting only a few hours a week to study is a great disadvantage, since the student forgets what he has learned from one period to the next. Some authorities recommend 10 hours a week as the "optimal minimum." We do not as yet know what the "optimal maximum" is, for experiments have not yet been conducted to determine when the law of diminishing returns sets in. It is believed that about 25 hours a week represents the optimal maximum.[14]

If then we assume that the student studies an hour a day for 5 days a week[15] and spends 2 hours a week doing homework, then it will take him a year to learn to speak (including also understanding), 4 years to speak and read, and 8 years to speak, read and write a foreign language. If, however, he spends 25 hours a week in the intensive study of a language, it will take him 8 to 9 weeks to learn to speak, 8 to 9 months to speak and read, and a year and a half to speak, read and write it.

Prospective immigrants and tourists who can devote two months to the intensive study of Hebrew before they leave on their trip, and while they are on their way to Israel, can learn to speak Hebrew by the time they reach the country. Even those who spend only a month on it can acquire enough of the rudiments of the language to understand and speak it to some extent when they arrive in Israel, and they will be able to improve their knowledge very quickly once they are there.

Is It Easier For an English Speaker to Learn Hebrew, or For a Hebrew Speaker to Learn English?

From what we have written so far it would appear that it does not take more time to learn Hebrew than it does to learn English. Is this actually so? English speakers consider Hebrew a difficult language to learn and English a very easy language. Experts in the teaching of English maintain that English is far easier to learn than any other language (except perhaps an artificial language like Esperanto). It should serve as the international language since "no other language in the world provides the same possibilities of word economy. . . . Providence seems to have singled out the English language for a special grace in this respect. It is unique. All other languages are inferior to it. . . ."[16]

The fact is that English has reached a remarkable degree of simplification. If we compare it with Hebrew we find that English has the following advantages:

1. By adding various prepositions and adverbs to a given

verb, it is possible to form verb phrases with different meanings. This is an enormous advantage on which Ogden based his Basic English, including 18 verbs only (see Chapter Four). Through addition of prepositions or adverbs the verb "go"—for example—yields in Basic English 21 different meanings for which Hebrew needs special semantic entities: go (ללכת), go about (להתעסק), go across (לעבור), go after (לעקוב), go against (להתנגד), go among (להתערב בתוך), go at (לתקוף), go before (להתקדם), go between (לתווך), go by (לחלוף), go down (לרדת), go from or out (לצאת), go in (להכנס), go off (להסתלק), go on (להמשיך), go over (לבדוק), go through (לסבול), go to (לגשת או לבקר), go under (לשקוע), go up (לעלות), go with (להתאים). Outside Basic English the possibilities of varying the meanings are even greater.

2. The fact that English is related to the Germanic languages and has a large Romance element makes it easy for German, Dutch, French, Spanish and Italian speakers to learn English. They recognize many cognates,[17] similar grammatical constructions, etc.

3. The fact that most Hebrew texts are unvocalized creates difficulty for the beginner.

4. The English noun is far simpler than the Hebrew noun with its two genders, dual form, different declensions, personal suffixes, etc.

5. The English verb has a simpler structure than the Hebrew verb with its seven conjugations and "conversive *Vav*."

6. The English cardinal numbers are far simpler than the Hebrew ones which have different forms when occurring before masculine or feminine nouns.

7. English does not add personal suffixes to its prepositions as does Hebrew.

On the other hand Hebrew has certain advantages over English:

1. Hebrew writing is phonetic as compared with the almost chaotic spelling of English. The student beginning English is rarely certain how to pronounce a word that he meets for the first time.

2. Hebrew does not have, as does English, two forms of letters—capital and small letters.

3. The Hebrew tense system is extremely simple, possessing three tenses as compared with the twelve English tenses with

their fine distinctions that prove the bane of advanced students as well as of beginners.

4. Hebrew does not have, as does English, many modal and aspectual verbal forms (subjunctive, progressive tenses, etc.).

5. The student of Hebrew does not have to devote time to "sequence of tenses" or "direct and indirect discourse"—features of English which take so much of the beginning student's time.

6. The structure of negative and interrogative sentences in Hebrew is very simple whereas in English they require considerable explanation and drill.

7. The relative conjunctions are simpler in Hebrew than in English where the student must learn how to use "who, whom, which, what, that, etc."

8. Though it is true that speakers of European languages will find very few cognates in Hebrew,[18] they do find many words which they recognize from the Prayerbook, religious observances, Yiddish, from what they have read about Zionism or Israel, etc.

9. The Hebrew vocabulary is far less extensive than the English. The number of roots is small. This is a great advantage for the student of Hebrew as compared with the student of English who has to learn to differentiate among various synonyms expressing the same general idea. Hebrew is also poor in idiomatic expressions as compared with English, where the wealth of idioms proves a stumbling block to the beginner.

We have attempted to list the features that make English easier for beginners and those that make Hebrew easier.[19] We could of course continue to add details, but the essential picture would not change. To return to our original question: Is English easier for the Hebrew speaker than Hebrew is for the English speaker? There is no doubt that if we were to ask Hebrew speakers they would tell us that Hebrew seems to them easier, and if we asked English speakers they would answer that English seems easier. Even if we tried to use objective criteria we would still find it difficult—or impossible—to decide which is the easier. But the important point for us here is that the difficulty of Hebrew has been greatly exaggerated. It may be assumed that Hebrew is not more difficult—or at most only a little more difficult—than English. Now English is considered an easy language, one which because of its simplicity is best qualified to serve as the international language. Hebrew can likewise serve as an international language for Jews in the Diaspora. We have already called attention to some of the features that make it easy to learn (easy pronunciation, lack of a case system, analytical character of its syntax, etc.).

What is required to spread Hebrew in the Diaspora is a corps of experienced teachers who keep abreast of advances in the field of language methodology. But it is equally important to encourage tendencies towards further simplification of Hebrew. Most of the immigrants coming to Israel know no Hebrew at all and it is important that we do everything in our power to make it easy for them to learn the language. Just as our ancestors during the Mishnaic period introduced many features which simplified the structure of Hebrew, so we today should welcome developments in present-day Hebrew which serve to make the language simpler and thus easier to learn.

Would the Use of the Latin Alphabet or of Fully Vocalized Texts Make It Easier to Learn Hebrew?

A suggestion made by the late Ittamar Ben-Avi and repeated by many others, including Arthur Koestler, is to substitute the Latin letters for the Hebrew, just as the Turks substituted the Latin alphabet for the Arabic. There is however a great difference. The Arabic alphabet was not appropriate for writing a non-Semitic language like Turkish, and the Arabic alphabet happens to be a very complicated one (there are, for example, four different forms for most of the letters depending on whether they occur separately, initially, medially or finally). Changing to the Latin alphabet proved a distinct advantage since there was now one letter—and only one—for each sound.

The Hebrew writing system, on the other hand, is basically a phonetic one. When one sees a Hebrew word one always knows how to pronounce it (except for some words where one would not be certain of the accent). On the other hand if one hears a word one is not always certain of the spelling since some Hebrew letters represent several sounds and, conversely, some sounds can be represented by several different letters (not to mention the fact that there are several "silent" letters).

Using the Latin alphabet for writing Hebrew would have serious disadvantages. It would no longer be possible to identify roots and thus to recognize related words.[20] The beginner may find it convenient to transcribe Hebrew words in the Latin alphabet until he masters the Hebrew alphabet, but he will soon find that in order to progress in his Hebrew studies he will have to learn the Hebrew writing system.

The Semitic peoples who invented the alphabet did not find it necessary, because of the structure of the Semitic languages, to indicate the vowels. But a system of indicating the vowels was worked out by the Massoretes, and it is used in elementary textbooks, books of poetry, in the case of difficult or foreign words, or in order to avoid ambiguity. Hebrew is usually written without a full indication of the vowels. Many people consider this a disadvantage and it has often been suggested that all Hebrew texts should be fully vocalized.

But is this really a disadvantage? There can be no doubt that it is inadvisable to give unvocalized texts to beginners; but on the other hand it would be equally inadvisable to vocalize texts for those who already know how to read Hebrew. The great role that roots and derivational patterns play in Hebrew makes it possible to indicate just the consonants (as is done in shorthand systems in other languages). This is not only a material advantage (saving composition costs and paper), but a psychological one as well. Studies of eye movements in reading have shown that the eye takes in not letters or words but whole groups of words. This means that when we read Hebrew our eye-span can take in more words than when we read English, and we can consequently read Hebrew faster.

We may conclude therefore that the substitution of the Latin alphabet for the Hebrew, or the use of fully vocalized texts, would not make the learning of Hebrew any easier, except in the initial stages.

The Importance of Emphasizing a Speaking Knowledge of Hebrew

During the period between the two world wars language teachers in high schools and colleges stressed the reading approach. Since language instruction had not proved very effective they decided to concentrate on developing a reading knowledge of a foreign language, so that the student could develop proficiency in at least one skill. They met with some measure of success: whereas formerly students had completed several years of language study with little to show for their efforts, they were now at least able to read simple texts in a foreign language. However, this was true only of students who studied the language for several years. Those who had studied only a year or two were not able to read even simple texts.

Under the influence of the Army language program in the

U. S. and Great Britain there has recently been a movement to stress a speaking knowledge of the foreign language. High schools in city school systems, private schools and colleges now attempt to secure language instructors who can teach their students to speak foreign languages. Smaller schools still devote all their attention to the reading aim.[21] It is now accepted practice to begin the study of a foreign language by first learning the pronunciation and "first aid expressions," and then passing on to reading. In fact some teachers now teach even Latin this way,[22] and with marked success. (This gives rise to a curious phenomenon: the study of Latin for centuries exercised a powerful influence on the study of modern languages, and now the process seems to have been reversed.)

The great interest which the Jews in the Diaspora are now taking in the Hebrew language, opens up the possibility that Hebrew may become their second language in the Diaspora. Those of us who are interested in the dissemination of Hebrew must take advantage of the best available ways and means to spread the knowledge of Hebrew. We must attempt to utilize whatever is important for our purpose in recent linguistic theory and methodology.[23] But above all we must define very clearly what our objectives are in teaching Hebrew, and we must direct all our efforts toward the achievement of the aims we set.[24]

We have now discussed various possible objectives. But defining our goal clearly is not the complete solution. It is equally important to determine by what stages we can progress towards our goal. As we have already pointed out, these stages should be:

First Stage—Speaking knowledge (including, of course, the ability to understand the spoken language)

Second Stage—Reading knowledge

Third Stage—Writing knowledge.

We should concentrate all our efforts in the beginning on the development of a speaking knowledge, for in this way we can achieve the practical and emotional objectives discussed earlier. The acquisition of a speaking knowledge should serve as an incentive for the student to continue his studies until he reaches the second stage, namely, the acquisition of a reading knowledge which will enable him to achieve the cultural objectives.

We must do everything in our power to encourage the teaching of spoken Hebrew in such schools in the Diaspora as can devote at least 200-250 hours to the study of Hebrew. This amount of time would of course not be sufficient to teach reading as well, except perhaps for rudimentary mechanical reading.

Our objective should be to teach all our students to speak Hebrew, many of them to speak and read, and some of the better ones to write as well as to speak and read. There is reason to believe that in this way we will have in the end more students who will be able to read and write Hebrew than we have now. It is only natural that students who have learned to speak Hebrew should have a strong incentive for learning to read and write it as well.

We have the good fortune to live during a period when Hebrew is taking its place as one of the modern languages. There can be no justification for continuing to teach Hebrew as though it were a dead language like Latin, Classical Greek, Aramaic, or Sanskrit. We must teach Hebrew in the same way we teach French or Spanish or any other modern language.

There have been in recent years three attempts to revive dead or dying languages, namely Gaelic, Hindustani,[25] and Hebrew. The 1949 Yearbook of Education[26] contains a discussion of the progress being made in these three languages. A. Marsh of Dublin University notes that only in certain of the remote country districts (Gaeltacht) has the Gaelic revival been successful, but that in Eire as a whole there has not been much success in making Gaelic an everyday spoken language despite the efforts of the government and the enthusiasm of the students. The writer is of the opinion that the pressure of English is too strong for the Gaelic revival to succeed. His conclusion is that "today there can be very few, if any, educationists in the country who do not believe that the future common language of Ireland is destined to be English."

S. K. Chatterji of Calcutta University points out that Hindustani serves as a lingua franca for some 250,000,000 people and is the third language in the world in terms of number of speakers, being surpassed only by Chinese and English. Yet little creative literature is being written in it. Such creative effort as there is in India finds expression in English. Professor Chatterji knows about the two other national linguistic experiments—the revival of Hebrew and Irish, "the success or failure of which we are watching with interest."[27]

In contrast to these two writers the author was able to state in his article (written at the beginning of the siege of Jerusalem and before the beginning of the mass immigration) that most of the Jewish inhabitants of Palestine and almost all of the younger generation can express themselves more freely in Hebrew than in any other language. Whereas the speech of the previous two generations was influenced by the literary language, today we find that spoken Hebrew is exerting more and more influence on its literary counterpart.

Learning to speak Hebrew creates a strong emotional tie with the Jewish nation in the past and present. It creates in the learner a desire to visit Israel and to seek out Hebrew-speaking circles in the Diaspora, to read the daily press and current Hebrew books, so that he may perfect his knowledge of the everyday spoken language. Nor will Hebrew educationalists whose first concern is to transmit Hebrew cultural values be disappointed. The knowledge of spoken Hebrew will strengthen the student's attachment to his people and their culture, and will induce him to pursue his studies further, to learn the Bible and the Hebrew literature of other periods, and even to learn to write Hebrew.

NOTES TO CHAPTER ONE

1. Bloomfield, L., *Language* (1933), p. 503.

2. Many articles on this subject are to be found in two periodicals published in New York: *Jewish Education* and *Sheviley Ha-Chinuch.*

3. See Bode, B. H., *Modern Educational Theories* (1927), p. 134, and Dewey, John, *The Sources of a Science of Education* (1929), p. 72.

4. See Katsh, A. I., "The Problems of Hebrew Education among Adolescent Jewish Students in the United States," *Ha-Chinuch Ha-Ivri Bitfutzot Ha-Golah* (1948), p. 91, cf. *Hebrew Language, Literature and Culture in American Institutions of Higher Learning* (1950). pp. 1-11.

5. Handschin, C. H., *Modern Language Teaching* (1940), p. 60.

6. See Lind, Melva, "Modern Language Learning: The Intensive Course as Sponsored by the United States Army and Implications for the Undergraduate Course of Study," *Genetic Psychology Monographs,* v. 38, 1948.

7. Bialik, Ch. N., "Machsorey Leshonenu Ve-Tikuna," *Dvarim Shebeal Pe* (Dvir, 1935), p. 136.

8. Lind, *op. cit.,* p. 38.

9. Handschin, *op. cit.,* p. 60.

10. See, e.g., Richards, I. A., *Basic English and its Uses* (1943), p. 67.

11. Lind, *op. cit.,* p. 16.

12. Duff, C., *How to Learn a Language* (1947), p. 93.

13. Several experiments have proved that adults have greater learning ability than adolescents or children. It has not been proved that linguistic aptitude is a function of age, but adults usually have more power of concentration and so are able to advance more rapidly in their studies. At all events Thorndike's experiments (reported in his *Adult Learning,* 1928) show that while children and adolescents learn to speak more rapidly than adults, the latter learn to read twice as fast as children. Buswell in his *Laboratory Study of the Reading of Modern Foreign Languages* (1927) compared the reading ability of adults with that of elementary school children and beginning high school students and found that reading ability develops with age. From the report of the Canadian Committee on Foreign Language Instruction we learn that college students progress twice as rapidly in learning a foreign language as high school students. Cf. Michael West, *On Learning to Speak a Foreign Language,* pp. 5-6.

We may conclude that while children surpass adolescents and adolescents surpass adults in ability to learn to speak a foreign language, adults are superior to adolescents and adolescents to children in their ability to learn to read and write.

14. Lind, *op. cit.*, p. 34.

15. We assume a school year of 30-40 weeks.

16. Duff, *op. cit.*, p. 20.

17. It has been estimated that 40-50% of the English vocabulary is cognate with French, German or Italian. See Handschin, *op. cit.*, p. 164.

18. English has borrowed a number of words from Hebrew (messiah, mammon, jubilee, cherub, cherubim, amen, shibboleth, seraph, etc.) but there are practically no cognates. For further information see Chapter Four on "The Vocabulary of Essential Hebrew," note 22.

19. One writer (Ralph Weiman, "The Re-Creation of Hebrew," *Commentary*, 1949, p. 565ff.) points out that there are many factors (simple phonetic structure, analytical syntactical structure, existence of a comparatively small number of roots with regular derivational patterns, etc.) which make it easy to learn to pronounce Hebrew and rapidly acquire a working vocabulary, but that the writing system (totally different alphabet from the one to which we are accustomed, use of unvocalized texts, etc.) is responsible for the impression many people have that Hebrew is a "difficult language."

20. The confusion would begin in the first lessons. The students would learn that the Hebrew form for "and" is *ve-* (written ו). Though this prefix is always written with the same letter (*Vav*), it has five different pronunciations depending on the phonetic context. There are a number of other Hebrew sounds which change according to phonetic environment (e.g., *basar* "meat" but *uvasar* "and meat"). However, the same letter is used in the Hebrew writing so that a beginner has no trouble in recognizing that *basar* and *vasar* are the same word. See Galanté, A., *L'Adoption des Caractères Latins*, Stanbul, Hüner Basimevi (1950).

21. *Encyclopedia of Modern Education*, ed. Harry N. Rivlin, (1950), p. 503.

22. Jones, P. M., "Proficiency in Languages," *Universities Quarterly*, v. 3 (1949), p. 694.

23. For a summary of recent methods, see: Friedl, B. C., *Principles and Techniques of Teaching Hebrew* (1950).

24. Jespersen considers the vagueness of objectives as the principal reason for our lack of success in foreign language teaching. See his *Mankind, Nation and Individual* (1946), p. 6.

25. Hindustani is of course a spoken language, so that the reference here is not to its revival as a spoken language but rather to the attempt on the part of the Indian intelligentsia to make Hindustani a cultural language that can take the place of English.

26. Published by Evans Bros. in association with the University of London Institute of Education. The articles are: Marsh, A., "The Revival of the Irish Language," pp. 157-166; Chatterji, S. K., "Language Problems in India," pp. 483-501; and Rieger, E., "The Revival of Hebrew," pp. 471-479.

27. Professor Chatterji mentions in his article that "the stress on Hebrew is a necessity in Palestine for the Jews, as it is attempting to combine Jews from different parts of Europe and Asia speaking different languages into a single speech unit. . . . But to what extent and in what manner a German or Polish or Spanish speaking boy or girl reacts to the use of only Hebrew in the classroom, the present writer has no information. Is Hebrew successful in replacing German or Polish or Spanish, or is it just used for decorative purposes? I must say that I was agreeably surprised to find two young Jewish students (one was a German speaker at home, and the other's language was Russian) talking to each other in fluent Hebrew, while traveling through Switzerland. . . ."

CHAPTER TWO

AWAY FROM THE BEATEN TRACK OF
HEBREW GRAMMAR

Revolutionary Ideas of Veteran Scholars

One of our veteran Hebrew teachers recently published an article entitled "Has Hebrew a Grammar?"[1] After a detailed analysis the author comes to the conclusion that modern Hebrew has no grammar. The grammatical structure of present-day Hebrew is extremely complicated, full of inner contradictions and has, as it were, more exceptions than rules. It is therefore necessary, in the opinion of the author, to reconstruct Hebrew grammar and make it conform to present-day pronunciation and usage by simplifying the rules and reducing the number of exceptions. We must sharply distinguish between the grammar of the Bible, which should be studied by itself, and the grammar of present-day Hebrew. Now is the appropriate moment to write a new Hebrew grammar based on current usage.

Revolutionary as this proposal may seem, it is in fact far from new. Many similar proposals have been made from the time that Hebrew was revived as a spoken language. Even Ahad Ha-Am, the late doyen of modern Hebrew literature, severely criticized those who wished to base Hebrew entirely on biblical usage and who looked upon the usages found in later literature as "mistakes."[2] Such critics, he argued, fail to take into account the fact that "grammar" is simply a description of the structure of a language at a given period. We have one system of grammar in the Bible, another in the Mishna,[3] and still another in Modern Hebrew. We ought to recognize that just as Mishnaic Hebrew represents a new development, so modern Hebrew represents a still newer stage, and a grammar of present-day Hebrew must take this fact into consideration. Ahad Ha-Am contended that grammarians should not try to correct imaginary errors but rather devote themselves to describing current usage. Bialik,[4] the late Hebrew "poet laureate,"

25

also looked upon so-called "grammatical mistakes" as unimportant. He pointed out that in a living language even illogicalities seem natural. Bialik believed that where grammatical changes have taken place we should adopt the latest stage in the development. Like Ahad Ha-Am he recognized that language grows and that we must take account of these developments. He sanctioned many of the changes which had taken place in spoken Hebrew, though he did not go as far in this regard as Klausner, for example.[5] The latter's proposals seemed extreme when they were first made. His principal suggestions were (a) to use the particle *shel* instead of the construct state, and *shel* plus the possessive suffixes instead of adding the possessive suffixes to the noun; (b) to eliminate the use of the *Vav* Conversive in prose usage; (c) to use adjectives in place of adverbs; (d) to use *yoter* to mark the comparative; and (e) to insert the definite article before the first (and not the second) term, when the construct state is used.

These proposals have found many supporters nowadays. Indeed some scholars wish to do everything possible to hasten these changes while Hebrew is still in a formative state. Professional grammarians, on the other hand, have opposed these suggestions as contrary to the basic structure of the language, but it seems likely that in a generation or two the opponents of the changes will have become accustomed to them and will wonder how they could have clung so long to obsolete and involved grammatical forms.

The Subjugation of Hebrew Grammar to Latin and Arabic Patterns

If we accept the well-known definition of grammar as "the mode in which words are connected in order to express a complete thought," then those modes are to be preferred which express an idea with the greatest simplicity and economy.

Language is in essence a democratic institution in that usage is determined by the majority. The task of the grammarian is not to devise rules but to analyze and describe the structure of the language at a given period. The efforts of grammarians to make language a logically perfect—and therefore normative—system have been at the root of our difficulties in language teaching. In dealing with a language we are dealing with an aspect of folk psychology; we do not have a completely logical structure but one with exceptions and contradictions, and with usages that arise and disappear very much as do fashions in dress.

A particular difficulty was created by the efforts of grammarians—including Hebrew grammarians—to make the grammar of the language they were describing correspond to Latin grammar. But Latin differs in so many important respects from the modern European languages that to delineate them in terms of Latin rules of grammar is to give a very false picture of their structure. This was true even in the case of a language so closely related to Latin as French. French and English philologists began to protest against this forcing of French and English into Latin molds,[6] and they called for a grammatical presentation based on the structure of the language in question without any reference to Latin. Since Latin was a dead language, grammarians could make hard-and-fast grammatical rules; but to attempt to do the same for the modern language was to ignore the fact that living languages are subject to change. This use of Latin as a model had disastrous effects, as we shall soon point out, on the grammatical treatment of Hebrew, particularly on the analysis of Hebrew syntax.

The development of Hebrew grammar has in general been influenced by foreign sources. Until the Gaonic period Hebrew grammar was limited to specific problems such as vocalization, differentiation of synonyms, etc. From the 10th century on it developed as a branch of Arabic grammar, and the work of Saadia Gaon, Hayyuj, Ibn Janah and others was influenced by Arabic. Semitic scholars who from the time of Reuchlin up to Gesenius continued to refine the grammatical presentation of Hebrew were influenced on the one hand by the structure of Arabic and on the other hand (consciously or unconsciously) by the structure of Latin.

We must cease delineating Hebrew in terms of Arabic or Latin and begin to analyze and record the structure of Hebrew as it is spoken and written today. Unless we do so we face the prospect that Hebrew may become stratified like Arabic, where we have three languages—classical Arabic, the semi-literary form (Koine) used in the newspapers and on the radio, and colloquial Arabic—which differ from one another as much as the various Romance languages differ from one another. Such a process can split national unity into upper and lower social classes and retard cultural progress, as we can witness also in India where there are three forms of language—classical Sanskrit, Prakrit, and colloquial Hindustani. It is important for us to take warning from the linguistic situation in India and in the Arabic-speaking world. We must strive for a uniform language in Israel and in the Diaspora, and for a grammar that reflects current usage.

Knowledge of Grammar Does Not Insure Correct Usage

Achad Ha-Am remarks in one of his essays[7] that knowing Hebrew grammar is one thing, using Hebrew correctly quite another. This fact has been recognized by all too few grammarians and teachers. Recent investigations have revealed how surprisingly little formal grammatical knowledge is necessary in order to speak or read a language.[8] One cannot of course have full command of a language without knowing the grammar well, but to speak or read a language one needs to know very little grammar. In order to learn to speak a language one has to listen to it as much as possible and to imitate what one hears. In order to learn to read a language one has to read extensively and to note matters of syntax, word usage, etc. The minute study of grammar may even have an adverse effect; if a teacher keeps stressing grammatical errors the students may end up by hesitating to speak the language at all, for fear that they may be making mistakes. Too much emphasis on grammar may inhibit the students from developing fluency in reading since they may pay more attention to grammatical features than to the content. The difficulty that many Germans have in speaking or writing a foreign language may be traceable to the over-emphasis on grammar and grammatical analysis in the German schools. Indeed one writer[9] attributes the rapid progress that children make in learning a language to the fact that they are not concerned about making mistakes. If one studies grammar, he will know grammar, but that does not mean that he will acquire a fluent command of the language or even be able to use it correctly.[10]

Recent research has borne out what was known empirically for a long time, namely, that the study of grammar has little effect on the correctness of the spoken and written usage of at least half the students, even if they are drilled in grammatical rules during the course of two years.[11] We are all acquainted with people who know all the grammatical rules and yet commit all sorts of mistakes in their speech and writing. One acquires correct usage not by memorizing rules but by imitating the best speakers and writers.

To be sure, it is easier to interest adults in grammatical analysis than it is to interest children or adolescents. Adults will listen to grammatical explanations more readily and will be better able to apply the grammatical information they learn.[12] But it is not wise to overburden them with grammar. They should be taught only such grammar as they will actually need in their everyday use of the language. The material should not be presented deductively but inductively. The teacher should point out a given grammatical feature each time it occurs and then at some point ask the student to induce from the examples that have been met the general principle involved.[13] There should be no memorizing of rules first and then applying them, as is customary with the deductive procedure, but practice by imitation should come first and making generalizations should follow in due course. Grammatical material learned in this way is far more likely to influence the students' usage than material presented deductively.

No less important than the question of how to teach grammar is the question of what to teach. Studies of the frequency of grammatical forms and constructions have been made for French, Spanish, German, etc.[14] Several studies along these lines have been begun in Hebrew and have shown, for example, that the *Kal* and *Hiphil* are the most common conjugations, that the sound roots and those ending in *He* are the most frequent ones, etc.[15] We now need a definitive study which can be used to determine which grammatical forms and constructions are the most essential and should be most stressed.

Frequency Count of Grammatical Errors

Several important attempts have been made in English to construct a functional grammar. As a guide to determining what to include, studies have been made of the most frequent errors in everyday usage. Such studies have a two-fold importance. If one has a list, say, of the 200 or 300 most common mistakes in spoken and written Hebrew, one has a guide as to what should be taught. One can divide this number over a specified number of years and concentrate each year on correcting a given number of errors. In an intensive course all this material can be covered in a number of months. If students acquire correct usage in regard to these 200 or 300 points they will have benefited more than they would by years of formal grammar. Frequency counts of errors have another importance as well. By studying the distribution of the errors, the teacher can discover the areas which present the greatest difficulty and center his efforts on them.

We have as yet no exhaustive study of common errors in Hebrew, but we do have a list compiled by several seminar groups in the School of Education of the Hebrew University on the basis of material collected by the Bet Sefer Reali in Haifa, by Professor Tur-Sinai in his commendable brochure *"Ha-Mivta Ha-Aliz,"* and by several students.[16]

For purposes of illustration we list here the 225 most common errors in everyday Hebrew. They are arranged in four groups: (A) Morphology; (B) Idiomatic Usage; (C) Syntax; (D) Vocalization. Most of the errors (138 in number) occur in the first group. The next highest number (56) is found in the second group.

A LIST OF THE 225 MOST COMMON ERRORS

A. Morphology

1. Prepositions	47
2. Adverbs	33
3. Verbs	16
4. Nouns	14
5. Conjunctions	10
6. Ordinal and Cardinal Numbers	6
7. Pronouns	6
8. Adjectives	6
Errors in Morphology	138
B. Errors in Idiomatic Usage	56
C. Errors in Syntax	18
D. Errors in Vocalization	13
Total	225

Correct Form   Incorrect Form

A. Morphology

Errors in the Use of Prepositions—47

The Preposition בְּ

ראובן עומד בגשם	1. ראובן עומד על הגשם
הקונה קשור בסוחר זה, או:	2. הקונה קשור עם סוחר זה
לסוחר זה	
גוענו ברעב ובצמא	3. גוענו מרעב ומצמא
צריך לגמור בדבר זה	4. צריך לגמור עם דבר זה
הרוסים נלחמו בגרמנים	5. הרוסים נלחמו נגד הגרמנים
הוא מסתכל בנוף	6. הוא מסתכל על הנוף
האיש הכה אותי במקל	7. האיש הכה אותי עם מקל
איני יכול לכתוב בעט	8. איני יכול לכתוב עם העט
אני לומד לכתוב במכונה	9. אני לומד לכתוב על מכונה
במי זה תלוי	10. ממי זה תלוי
אני שבע רצון בו (מרוצה בו)	11. אני שבע רצון ממנו (מרוצה ממנו)
החיילים צדדו בזכות המנהיג הזה	12. החיילים צדדו את המנהיג הזה
אסע ברכבת הצהרים	13. אסע עם רכבת הצהרים

The Preposition אֶת

אל תפריע אותי	14. אל תפריע בעדי
אל תמנע אותי לעשות זאת	15. אל תמנע בעדי לעשות זאת
נקטתי את האמצעים החדשים האלה	16. נקטתי באמצעים החדשים האלה
זה כתוב בחומש	17. בחומש כתוב את זה
היתה להם היכולת	18. היתה להם את היכולת
אמרתי אותו דבר	19. אמרתי את אותו דבר
ראיתי את יוסף	20. ראיתי יוסף
את ידידי (או: לידידי) קרה אסון	21. עם ידידי קרה אסון

The Preposition עַל

יוסף התגעגע על משפחתו	22. יוסף התגעגע אל משפחתו
ידעתי על דבר זה	23. ידעתי מדבר זה
האב ספר לבנו על אודות (או: על)	24. האב ספר לבנו אודות המקרה
המקרה	
עבודה זו נמאסה עלי מזמן רב	25. עבודה זו נמאסה לי מזמן רב
אני מודה לך על המתנה	26. אני מודה לך בעד המתנה
תודה לך על העצה	27. תודה לך בשביל העצה
תודה. התשובה: על לא דבר	28. תודה. התשובה: אין בעד מה

The Preposition לְ

29. הוא מחכה עלי	הוא מחכה לי
30. הוא קורא אותי	הוא קורא לי
31. אדם אחראי בעד מעשיו	אדם אחראי למעשיו
32. צחקתי ממנו	צחקתי לו
33. לעגתי ממנו	לעגתי לו
34. הנאשם שקר את השופט	הנאשם שקר לשופט
35. נשק אותי	נשק לי
36. אני צריך את הספר	אני צריך לספר
37. בקשר עם מכתבי מאתמול	בקשר למכתבי מאתמול

Various Prepositions

38. סביבי	סביבי
39. תַּחְתּוֹ	תַּחְתָּיו
40. בלעדְךָ	בלעדָיךָ
41. אֲליכם, אֲליהם	אֲליכם, אֲליהם
42. מִמְּכֶם, מִמְּכָן, מֵהֶם	מִכֶּם, מִכָּן, מֵהֶם
43. אִתָּךְ	אִתָּךְ
44. בשבילָנו	בשבילָנו
45. אצלָנו, אצלָהֶם	אצלָנו, אצלָם
46. בין אחי ואחותי	בין אחי לאחותי או: בין אחי ובין אחותי
47. עבור	בעבור

Errors in the Use of Adverbs—33

1. לנקד טוב	לנקד היטב
2. אני מכיר די יפה	אני מכיר יפה למדי
3. לרגלי החג באו תירים	לרגל החג באו תירים
4. נכנסתי להצגה בחנם	נכנסתי להצגה חנם
5. גם היום באת לחנם	גם היום באת חנם
6. הייתי שמה	הייתי שם
7. בוא להנה	בוא הנה
8. הנה ושוב	הלוך ושוב, או: הנה והנה
9. איך שמוֹ	מה שמו
10. איך קוראים לזה בעברית	מה קוראים לזה בעברית
11. הֻכְסַף שולם למפרע	הכסף שולם מראש

הוא לא ישוב עוד	12. הוא לא ישוב יותר
כבר בשנה שעברה	13. עוד בשנה שעברה
כשאקרא תקום	14. כשאקרא אז תקום
בלבלת לי את המוח די והותר	15. מספיק בלבלת לי את המוח
כמה לפי השעון שלך	16. כמה על השעון שלך
פחות	17. יותר פחות
יותר	18. יותר הרבה
אם כן אבוא מחר	19. אז אבוא מחר
הוא בודאי יבוא	20. הוא בטח יבוא
שוב, או: עוד פעם	21. שוב פעם
לא כלום	22. כלום
בני עדיין לא בא	23. בני עוד טרם בא
לאן הלכת	24. איפה הלכת
איפה היית	25. איה היית
מעולם לא היית שם	26. לעולם לא היית שם
לא אשלם לך לעולם	27. לא אשלם לך מעולם
אני אוהב אותם ביותר	28. אני אוהב אותם הכי הרבה
אני מפגר ביותר	29. אני מפגר הכי
ברגל	30. רגלי
אל תתן את הספר אף לאחד	31. אל תתן את הספר לאף אחד
לא שמעתי אף מאדם אחד, או: לא שמעתי מאיש	32. לא שמעתי מאף אדם אחד
קבלתי מכתב עוד מעיר אחת וגם כתבתי עוד לעיר אחת	33. קבלתי מכתב מעוד עיר אחת וגם כתבתי לעוד עיר אחת

Errors in the Use of Verbs—16

לויתי ממנו כסף	1. הלויתי ממנו כסף
שכרתי אצלו חדר	2. השכרתי אצלו חדר
שלמה הכה אותה; הבנין נבנה לפני שנה	3. שלמה הכה אותה; הבנין נבנה לפני שנה
ישחט	4. ישחט
עוזבי	5. עוזבי
מוצאת	6. מוצאת
חותכת, שופכת	7. חותכת, שופכת
שן	8. יושן
ישן, נקן	9. ישן, נקן

גְּדֵלִים, חֲדֵלִים	10. גוֹדְלִים, חוֹדְלִים
נָשִׁים	11. נְשִׁים
אָחֲשֹׁב, אֶעֱבֹד, אֶעֱזֹב	12. אַחשׁב, אַעבד, אַעזב
הֶעָו, הֶעָוָה	13. הֶעָיו, הֶעָיוה
דֵעָה מוּטְעֵית	14. דעה מוטעת
הַשִּׁינָה הִיא דבר חשוב, אוֹ : הַשִּׁינה דבר חשוב	15. הַשִּׁינה הוא דבר חשוב
רְאִיתֶם, שְׁמַעְתֶּם, נְסַעְתֶּם	16. רָאִיתֶם, שָׁמַעְתֶּם, נָסַעְתֶּם

Errors in the Use of Nouns—14

כוס שניה	1. כוס שֵׁנִי
שרות מהיר	2. שרות מהירה
עט נובע	3. עט נובעת
אפנים גדולים ; מכנסים ארוכים	4. אפנים גדולות; מכנסים ארוכות
קָשָׁיִים	5. קָשָׁיִים
חוֹף–חוֹפִים	6. חוֹף–חָפִּים
שְׂמָחוֹת	7. שְׂמָחוֹת
עֲגָלוֹת	8. עֲגָלוֹת
אדוניו גרש אותו	9. אדונו גרש אותו
בית זה נעזב ע״י בעליו	10. בית זה נעזב ע״י בעלו
מקום מגוּרֵיהם	11. מקום מגורם
סִפְרֵיכֶם, סִפְרֵיהֶם	12. סְפָרֵיכֶם, סְפָרֵיהֶם
צַבָּע	13. צַבָּעִי
בית־הספר	14. הבית־ספר

Errors in the Use of Conjunctions—10

אילו היה לי כסף	1. אם היה לי כסף
אפילו היתה דעה זו נכונה...	2. אפילו אילו היתה דעה זו נכונה...
מפני שירד גשם, לא יכולתי לבוא	3. היות שירד גשם, לא יכולתי לבוא
מפני ששמע	4. למה ששמע

אראה לך את המקום שבו תשב, או: אראה לך איפה לשבת	5. אראה לך איפה שתתשב
תלך, כשנאמר לך	6. תלך, מתי שנאמר לך
ראיתי אותו כשצחק	7. ראיתי אותו מתי שצחק
מפני שאני עסוק	8. בעד זה שאני עסוק
כשבאו; משבאו	9. איך שהם באו
כל כמה שסבלו, לא בכו, או: אף על פי שסבלו הרבה, לא בכו	10. כמה שסבלו, לא בכו

Errors in the Use of the Ordinal and Cardinal Numbers—6

שבע פעמים	1. שבעה פעמים
אחד עשר פועלים	2. אחת עשרה פועלים
אחת עשרה פועלות	3. אחד עשר פועלות
שנים-עשר או: שתים-עשרה, ששה-עשר או: שש-עשרה	4. שנים-עשרה, ששה עשרה
תשיעי, שביעי	5. תישעי, שיבעי
שעה ושלשה רבעים, או שעה ושלשת רבעי שעה	6. שעה ושלשת רבעי

Errors in the Use of Pronouns—6

ילדה זאת, או: הילדה הזאת	1. הילדה הזאתי
ילדה זו	2. ילדה זו
הכֹּל אומרים	3. כֻּלָּם אומרים
הלכתי לבדי הביתה	4. הלכתי בעצמי הביתה
בשנה שעברה	5. בשנה העברה
תעזרו זה לזה	6. תעזרו אחד לשני

Errors in the Use of Adjectives—6

קצָר, שפָל	1. קצָר, שפָל
הוא גדול ממני	2. הוא יותר גדול ממני
הוא הטוב בכתה	3. הוא הכי טוב בכתה
הוא הטוב ביותר	4. הוא הכי טוב
טוב יותר	5. יותר טוב
תמונה זו יפה מזו	6. תמונה זו יותר יפה כמו זו

B. Errors in the Use of Idioms—56

חשכו עיני או: חשך עולמי	1. נעשה לי חושך בעינים
הוא מציק לי מאד, או: הוא מציק לי עד מות	2. הוא עושה לי את המות
להשיב תשובה	3. לתת תשובה
לערוך את השולחן	4. להכין את השולחן
להסביר	5. לתת להבין
אינני מעריך אותו	6. אינני מחזיק ממנו
זה לא יקום, או: זה לא יצא לפועל	7. זה לא ילך
איפה אנו עומדים	8. איפה אוחזים
אני חוזר בי מדברי	9. אני לוקח בחזרה את דברי
זה ימשך זמן רב, או: זה יארך	10. זה יקח הרבה זמן
הארוחה לא נעמה לי, או: לא היתה טעימה לי	11. הארוחה לא מצאה חן בעיני
הוא משתכר 50 ל"י לחודש	12. הוא מרויח 50 ל"י לחודש
זכיתי במשחק	13. הרוחתי במשחק
הוא מושך אותי בשערות (הכוונה כאן למשיכה ולא לסחיבה שפירושה גרירה על פני הקרקע)	14. הוא סוחב אותי בשערות
עצור	15. עמוד
האוטובוס נעצר	16. האוטובוס נעמד
השאלתי לו את הספר	17. הלויתי לו את הספר
שאלתי את הספר	18. לויתי את הספר
אני אוכל הרבה מאד	19. אני אוכל המון
בליל שבת נפסקת תנועת האו-טובוסים	20. בליל ששי נפסקת תנועת האו-טובוסים
יהודי בעל זקן	21. יהודי עם זקן
השחקן עלה על הבימה	22. השחקן עלה על הבמה
באתי להרשם בבית-הספר	23. באתי להתרשם בבית-הספר
המעיל תלוי בארון	24. המעיל תולה בארון
ימאס עלי	25. ימאס לי
הנח לי	26. עזוב אותי
שכבנו לישון	27. הלכנו לישון
הפקיד רצה להוסיף לשבת במשרדו, או: להמשיך לשבת במשרדו	28. הפקיד רצה לשבת הלאה במשרדו
מה שמך?	29. איך קוראים לך?

התלוצץ, או: ספר הלצה	30. עשה הלצה
העיר עלולה ליפול כל רגע	31. העיר יכולה ליפול כל רגע
חילים שעתה זה באו מהחזית	32. חילים שרק זה באו מהחזית
עליתי לקומה השניה	33. הלכתי למעלה לקומה השניה
לנעוץ מסמרים	34. לדפוק מסמרים
הוא חושש שמא ירד גשם	35. הוא מפחד שמא ירד גשם
יוסף היה לפנים שחקן טוב	36. יוסף היה פעם שחקן טוב
גנב ממני את הארנק	37. גנב לי את הארנק
הרכיב משקפים	38. לבש משקפים
נעל נעלים	39. לבש נעלים
חבש כובע	40. לבש כובע
פקח את עיניו	41. פתח את עיניו
עצם את עיניו	42. סגר את עיניו
חלץ את נעליו	43. פשט את נעליו
בית של שתי קומות	44. בית משתי קומות
ספר של שני חלקים	45. ספר משני חלקים
מעות	46. כסף קטן
תגיד לו זאת בשמי	47. תגיד לו זאת ממני
הוא מציר את תמונתי	48. הוא מציר תמונה ממני
הניח את הדלת פתוחה	49. עזב את הדלת פתוחה
משקל התינוק 5 ק"ג	50. התינוק שוקל 5 ק"ג
אבד לי ספר	51. אבדתי ספר
הבית נבנה בידי פועלים יהודים	52. הבית נבנה עם פועלים יהודים
השמלה אינה הולמת אותי	53. השמלה אינה מתאימה לי
ילד אחד מכה את חברו	54. ילד אחד מכה את השני
גם בגולה וגם בארצנו לא היו	55. לא בגולה ולא בארצנו לא היו
היתה לנו ברירה בין בריחה	56. היו לנו שתי ברירות: אחת —
להתקפה, או: היו לנו שתי	בריחה ואחת — התקפה
אפשרויות, אחת — בריחה	
ואחת — התקפה	

C.   Errors in Syntax—18

המדריך הוביל אותנו לסמטאות, לבתי כנסת ולכותל המערבי	1. המדריך הוביל אותנו לסמטאות, בתי כנסת והכותל המערבי
כך אמר אברהם	2. כך אברהם אמר
מה קוראים לזה בעברית	3. מה בעברית קוראים לזה
וזה הועיל הרבה	4. וזה הרבה הועיל
תלמידי בית־הספר ומוריו, או: התלמידים והמורים של בית־ הספר	5. תלמידי ומורי בית־הספר
החיבור מלא שגיאות; אני מכוסה זיעה	6. החיבור מלא עם שגיאות; אני מכוסה עם זיעה
השולחן עשוי ברזל	7. השולחן עשוי מברזל
כשבאו וראו, ברחו	8. שבאו וראו, ברחו
יוסף נבחן גם באנגלית, או: יוסף נבחן באנגלית גם כן	9. יוסף נבחן באנגלית גם
גם אני רוצה ללכת, או: אני גם כן רוצה ללכת	10. אני גם רוצה ללכת
אבל אני הייתי הראשון	11. אני אבל הייתי הראשון
איזה דבר שהוא	12. איזה שהוא דבר
כמובן הלכתי לקונצרט, או: מובן שהלמכתי לקונצרט	13. כמובן שהלכתי לקונצרט
כנראה שניתם את דעתכם, או: נראה ששניתם את דעתכם	14. כנראה ששניתם את דעתכם
אין לי הספר	15. אין לי את הספר
יש לי הספר	16. יש לי את הספר
זה כתוב בחומש	17. בחומש כתוב את זה
היתה להם היכולת	18. היתה להם את היכולת

D.   Errors in Vocalization—13

בְּנָאי, רְשָׁאי, וְדָאי, זַכַּאי	1. בְּנָאִי, רְשָׁאִי, וְדָאִי, זַכָּאִי
נֶדֶר	2. נֶדֶר
מְכַשְׁפה	3. מַכְשֵׁפה
פְּרֵדה	4. פְּרֵדה
וּבַבית	5. וְבַּבית
וּמַה	6. וְמַה
מְחַרְתִים, אֱמָנוּת, אָמְנָם, תָּכְנִית,	7. מָחֳרתים, אֲמָנוּת, אָמְנָם, תָכְנית,
(צריך לבטא o)	צָהֳרים (מבטאים a)
(צריך לבטא a)	8. צָרְפת (מבטאים o)

הָאָרֶץ	9. הָאָרֶץ
שדרות	10. שדרות
שקט שורר	11. שקט שורר
צרכי ציבור	12. צרכי ציבור
(צריך לבטא בפתח גנובה)	13. אלוה, גבוה, תמה

The list given here does not include all the mistakes but merely the more serious ones. A number of items are not included here because we felt that though they are often labeled "mistakes," they are on the way towards becoming established in the language. "Mistakes" of this sort sometimes represent new developments which may serve to enrich the language or make it more flexible.[17] To give an example, we did not include the use of טרם in the sense of עדין לא (e.g. בני טרם בא) though this is a "mistake" according to Biblical usage.[18] Expressions like טרם בא are used by the best journalists and writers. On the other hand, we have listed עוד טרם (for example בני עוד טרם בא) as a mistake. Or to cite another example, we all know that expressions like אני כן אלך or אני לא אלך are translations from Yiddish and that it is more idiomatic to use ודאי אלך or some similar expression. But this use of כן or לא for purposes of emphasis is so popular and widespread (even among the best speakers) that it is questionable whether it ought to be included in the list of errors. This same is true of other expressions which are translations of Yiddish idioms, as for example ראשי כואב instead of אני חש בראשי Similarly we have not listed a number of adjectives like חוצפני (for עקשן (for קשה , etc.).[19] (מחוצף) for כשרוני (for מוכשר)

We may cite one more example. In speech and even in writing comparatively few people use the interrogative or an interrogative particle (e.g. ?ההולך אתה or ?כלום אתה הולך). The question mark serves to indicate a question in writing and the question intonation serves the same purpose in speech. We have here a development which helps to simplify the language and we have not therefore included the dropping of the interrogative particles in the list of errors.

The list we have given represents a random sampling and contains the most common errors. The syntactical errors listed probably represent a relatively small proportion of the actual errors, but we do not, as we shall soon point out, have any satisfactory frequency count to guide us. Though the present list must be regarded as merely provisional until such a count is made, it represents the result of more than ten years' work. It is based on studies made during the years 1936-1949 (with an interruption of two years) by students in the School of Education of the Hebrew University. Each student spent a week listening to the speech around him—on the street, in buses, in restaurants and cafes, etc. — and jotted down all the errors he could detect. When the material was classified it was discovered that conventional Hebrew grammar does not reflect many important aspects of everyday spoken Hebrew. We need however a basic study of the subject before we can determine how reliable our list actually is.

Prepositions, Adverbs and Conjunctions Are the Real Troublemakers

The reader will discover, perhaps to his surprise, that 90 errors out of the 225 listed concern prepositions, adverbs and conjunctions.

On the other hand there are only 43 errors that have to do with nouns, verbs or matters of vocalization. If we consider the nature of the commonest errors, it is obvious that our students do not need more formal grammar but rather more practice in using correct forms. This is particularly true of vocalization; most of the mistakes are made as frequently by those who have studied vocalization as by those who have not. In order to know that one says מְכַשֵּׁף‎, פְּרָדה‎, שׁוֹרֵר‎ etc. and not שׁוֹרֵר‎ or פְּרָדה‎, מְכַשֵּׁף‎ one does not need to study the general principles of vocalization but rather to have one's attention directed to these specific words. Anyone familiar with grammatical instruction in our schools knows how much time is spent on the verb, noun and the theory of vocalization, and how little time is devoted to prepositions, conjunctions and articles, which, as we have just seen, prove the real stumbling block. Teachers and textbook writers must come to recognize the vital role that prepositions, adverbs and conjunctions play in our language and must place more emphasis upon them and less upon nouns and verbs. Similar conclusions have been reached for English.[20] They are the rock bottom of the basic vocabulary and of the frequency lists.

Idiomatic Usage to Be Cultivated

Errors in idiomatic usage comprise another important area. In our list, 56 mistakes (a quarter of the total number) were mistakes in idioms. Most of these errors arise as literal translations from Yiddish or, in the case of the Arabic-speaking Jews, from Arabic. The teacher must impress upon his students the importance of idiomatic usage, for idioms give the language its particular individuality and flavor. The teacher must not confine himself to the minutiae of grammatical analysis but rather try to cultivate in his students a feeling for good Hebrew style.

Syntax Is of Prime Importance

Practically all our attention in grammatical instruction has been concentrated on problems of morphology and very little on problems of syntax. The unit of expression, however, is not the word but the sentence, and the exact meaning of a word is determined by the context of the complete sentence in which it stands. Morphology deals with the different forms a word may assume, with declensions and conjugations, with prefixes and suffixes; syntax deals with the way words are organized into a sentence. In morphology one can set up hard-and-fast rules and there is little room for individual variations. In syntax, on the other hand, we have more choice; we can often organize a sentence in more than one way and there is more room for individual variations. Languages differ more in morphology than in syntax.[22] For example, Latin differs considerably from the other European languages in that the Latin verb has a hundred and twenty-five inflectional forms,[23] but it does not differ from them so greatly in syntax.

It has been customary to distinguish between synthetic languages like Latin and Arabic, and analytic languages like English (and also in a great measure Hebrew). In the synthetic languages the word is the important unit, and the meaning centers, as it were, on the individual word. In the analytic languages, on the contrary, it is the sentence that is important, and the meaning depends to a great extent on word order, emphasis, and the rhythm of the sentence. In the historical development of languages there seems to be a tendency from the synthetic to the analytic, and it appears that languages are likely to become more and more analytic in the future.[24] English is one of the best examples of a language which in the course of its history has developed from a synthetic to a highly analytic language. In contrast to the synthetic languages where differentiations of meaning are expressed by modifications within the body of the word, the analytic languages express differences of meaning through syntactic rearrangement. Analytic languages, although "poor" in inflectional forms, are in no way inferior to the synthetic languages in their ability to express concepts and ideas: they simply use more dynamic means. The English word order is as potent a means of expression as is the Latin use of suffixes. There is here no question of functional poverty, but of formal economy.[25]

The early Hebrew grammarians attempted to describe Hebrew syntax in terms of Arabic or Latin, both of which are synthetic languages. As a result the structure of the Hebrew sentence became compressed and rigid. The Hebrew writers who lived in Europe and were influenced by the study of Latin introduced into Hebrew the Latin sentence structure with its main and subordinate clauses, etc. But Hebrew syntax was originally very free; word unit was placed beside word unit, and the connection between them was often inferred from the context rather than explicitly expressed. In technical terms Hebrew syntax was paratactic, that is, sentences, clauses and phrases were placed together, often without any conjunctive word. This paratactic nature of Hebrew syntax has many advantages,[26] one of the most important of which is that the learner has far less difficulty with Hebrew syntax than with Latin syntax, for example, or the syntax of many of the European languages. Until the Haskalah period Hebrew was for the most part paratactic in structure. When a Hebrew speaker said מצא אשה מצא טוב or יוסיף דעת יוסיף מכאוב he did not find it necessary to indicate which was the main clause and which was subordinate, nor did he find it necessary to add conjunctions; the connection of the word units was clear enough from the context. In the European languages he would have to say "When one finds a woman, he finds a good thing" or "If a man increases knowledge, he increases sorrow." By introducing "when" or "if" we indicate the main clause and the subordinate one, but we do not make the meaning any clearer or more precise.

We may cite here from the Mishna a typical example illustrating the original paratactic structure of Hebrew:

דיני ממונות בשלושה 1

זה בורר לו אחד 2

וזה בורר לו אחד 3

ושניהם בוררים להן עוד אחד 4

דברי רבי מאיר 5

וחכמים אומרים 6

שני דייינין בוררין להן עוד אחד 7

זה פוסל דיינו של זה 8

וזה פוסל דיינו של זה 9

דברי רבי מאיר 10

וחכמים אומרים, אימתי 11

מביא עליהן ראיה שהן קרובין 12

We can see the Latin-European influences, which are syntactic rather than paratactic, by rendering the passage into current Hebrew as follows:

דיני ממונות נידונים בשלושה דיינים 1

רבי מאיר סבור כי כל אחד משני הצדדים בורר לו דיין אחד 2
ושניהם בוררים להם את השלישי, ואילו לדעת החכמים
בוררים שני הדיינים את השלישי

רבי מאיר סבור כי כל אחד משני הצדדים 3
רשאי לפסול את דיינו של יריבו,
ואילו לדעת החכמים אין להתיר זאת אלא אם כן
מוכיח צד אחד שהדיין הוא קרובו של הצד השני

A comparison of the above passage in its Mishnaic original and its tentative current version shows that what the Mishna expressed tersely in a loose structure of twelve coordinated units, would be rendered in current Hebrew style by three sentences, of which the last two are main clauses containing several subordinate clauses.

It is important to encourage the freer, paratactical structure of Hebrew. On the one hand, we shall be approaching closer to the earlier structure of the language, and on the other, we shall be making the study of Hebrew syntax far easier for the beginner. We have previously emphasized that our grammar teachers ought to devote more time to the study of prepositions, adverbs and conjunctions, to the study of idiomatic usage and to the correction of the commonest errors. Here we may emphasize the importance of not concentrating solely on the study of morphological forms but of devoting considerable time to sentence structure and rhythm of current Hebrew. Hebrew is a relatively uninflected language which expresses important grammatical relationships by means of word order.

The teaching of Hebrew grammar has to be considered anew by our grammarians, language teachers and textbook writers, and our present course of study needs to be radically revised.

NOTES TO CHAPTER TWO

1. Yitzhak Livni in *Molad,* No. 17-18, 1949 (in Hebrew).

2. Achad Ha-Am, "The Language and its Grammar," *Al Parashat Derachim* (Berlin, 1921), v. 1.

3. It is interesting to note that this problem also existed in the period of the Mishna and Talmud. When it was pointed out that in the Bible the plural of "ewe" is רחלים but in the current usage רחלות , Rabbi Jochanan explained that biblical usage is one thing and current usage another (Chulin, 137).

4. Bialik was well versed in philological matters. Nevertheless the grammarian Avrounin has pointed out numerous grammatical errors in Bialik's writings. It is interesting to recall that Pope found many errors in Shakespeare's works, and indeed in every generation grammarians have discovered grammatical errors in the writings of the best authors. See C. C. Fries, *The Teaching of English* (1949), p. 26.

5. Klausner, Joseph, *Short Grammar of Modern Hebrew* (1935) (in Hebrew).

6. For generations English grammarians vied with one another in an attempt to describe English grammar entirely in terms of Latin grammar. They went so far as to take over the entire Latin case system despite the fact that English as a matter of fact has no cases at all.

7. Achad Ha-Am, *op. cit.,* v. 1.

8. Handschin, *op. cit.,* p. 88.

9. Duff, *op. cit.,* p. 15.

10. *Ibid.,* p. 29.

11. *Encyclopedia of Modern Education,* p. 532.

12. Fries, C. C., *The Teaching and Learning of English as a Foreign Language* (1950), p. 35.

13. Cheydleur studied the effectiveness of the deductive and inductive methods of presenting grammatical information, and found that information acquired inductively was retained two and a half times longer and that teachers had to spend 12 times as many hours in correcting errors in the compositions of students who had studied grammar deductively. See Handschin, *op. cit.,* p. 148.

14. *Encyclopedia of Modern Education,* p. 534.

15. Gabrieli, N., *Ketav Vesefer Bevet Hasefer* (1949), p. 298.

16. The most important studies are those of Solomon Mirkin-Morag (*Al Shibushey Halashon Vedarchey Akiratam, Ha-Chinuch,*

1947), Pinheas Wollman-Tsamri (*Hasignon Haivri Vetikuney Shibushim Balashon;* this study lists about a thousand mistakes), and Aviad Yafe (*Osef Shgiot Mipi Hashmua Vehakatuv*).

17. Tur-Sinai, N. H., *Halashon Vehasefer* (1948), p. 337ff.

18. We find the word *terem* used in the Bible with a future tense but with a past meaning.

19. Bialik protested against this use of *akshan,* which he identified with the root in *ikesh* which has the opposite meaning. *Akshan* in current speech means "stubborn" whereas *ikesh* means "a perverse or fickle person." Bialik once told the author that his grandmother always used *kashe* in speaking of a difficult or stubborn person but that his mother used *akshan* instead and he thought that the misuse of *akshan* might have arisen in the generation between his grandmother and mother. We do not find *akshan* in the older Hebrew literature. Joseph Aharonowitz, with whom I once discussed the matter, was of the opinion that the usage first arose in Yiddish where the saying *Stam makshan am haaretz* was corrupted to *stam akshan am haaretz.*

20. See Richards, *op. cit.,* p. 49f. Ogden in his Basic English calls the little words "operators." Chase calls them "sticks of dynamite" and compares them with electrons and atoms in modern physics.

21. Bialik, "Kodesh Vachol Balashon," *Dvarim Beal Pe,* Part II (1935), p. 128.

22. Bloomfield, *op. cit.,* p. 207.

23. *Ibid,* p. 223.

24. Sapir, E., *Language: An Introduction to the Study of Speech* (1921), p. 135f.

25. *Ibid,* p. 65f.

26. Ahad Ha-Am, for all his linguistic attainments, failed to recognize that it was impossible to imitate in Hebrew the syntactical structure of Latin or the European languages which are similar to Latin in their syntax. In his essay "The Language and Its Grammar" (Al Parashat Derachim, v. 1) he writes that "Renan in his *Histoire du peuple d'Israel* justly remarks that the greatest fault of the Semitic people is that the verbal system they created cannot express many nuances of tense and mode; to this very day Arabic speakers have to struggle with this problem. . . . Anyone familiar with European languages is constantly aware of the fact that the main difficulty in using Hebrew is not so much the poverty of the vocabulary as the poverty of morphological forms."

We can scarcely accept his judgment today. The wealth of temporal and modal forms in the European languages does not necessarily make for greater clarity and precision, and, needless to say, they impose a heavy burden on the learner.

CHAPTER THREE

WAYS AND MEANS TO A UNIFIED HEBREW PRONUNCIATION

The Role of Phonetics

Up until now we have been accustomed, in the teaching of Hebrew, to concentrate on vocabulary and grammar—that is, on the meaning or semantic aspect. In reviving Hebrew as a spoken language we have made great strides forward in the field of semantics but have done very little in the field of phonetics. Comparatively few people in Israel take pains with their pronunciation, and consequently the Hebrew pronunciation one commonly hears leaves much to be desired.

Modern Hebrew pronunciation tends to be careless and little attention is paid to the esthetic aspect. Those who take care to pronounce Hebrew well are often considered as pedantic or affected. Even in the Hebrew theatre one often hears actors whose Hebrew has a Russian, German or other accent. Few teachers really make an effort to correct and to improve the faulty Hebrew pronunciation of their students.

In addition to the esthetic considerations, there are also very practical ones. One who pronounces a language correctly and who articulates clearly is understood even if he makes many grammatical mistakes. On the other hand, one who has a poor pronunciation will often find that even though he has an excellent command of grammar his listeners will find his speech unintelligible. This holds equally true for understanding spoken language: One who has given attention to pronunciation will be able to follow rapid speech even though his vocabulary may be limited and his knowledge of the grammar meager. Conversely, one who has not paid attention to the pronunciation of a new language will find that he is not able to follow the simplest conversation, even though he may know thousands of words and know the grammar of the language thoroughly. Moreover, one who learns the pronunciation properly develops a "language sense" that stands him in good stead even if his goal is merely a reading knowledge of the language. The importance of phonetics is so great that many language experts consider phonetic instruction absolutely essential in language teaching. One of them has expressed the opinion that "pronunciation is of at least twice as much importance as grammar!"[1]

Language does not have as its sole function the communication of ideas. The social function of language is equally important. Human beings find it difficult to endure silence. A prolonged silence among a group of people will create uneasiness and tension. A person who keeps silent too long is suspected of being conceited or hostile. In a word, the purpose of language is not always the communication of specific ideas or information. Very often we talk simply for the sake of talking or in order to create a friendly social atmosphere.[2]

A particular aura of feeling surrounds a pleasant or an unpleasant pronunciation. People are often influenced not so much by what a man says as they are by his personality as revealed through his pronunciation and intonation. To be sure, there is nothing that can do so much to create a spirit of unity and cooperation between the Jews of the Diaspora and those in Israel as the ability to converse in Hebrew or at least to exchange a few words in Hebrew. But a common language is not enough; both groups must have a common pronunciation and intonation if there is to be an atmosphere of ease and equality.

The First Maxim in Language Learning: Listen Carefully!

It is important to begin the study of Hebrew with pronunciation exercises. In the first stage of teaching a language the emphasis should be on phonetics. Only later should the attempt be made to increase the student's vocabulary. In the first lessons—some maintain in the first thirty hours of instruction[3]—a student should confine himself to a limited vocabulary and concentrate on achieving correct pronunciation within this vocabulary.[4] It is not an easy task to acquire correct pronunciation of a new language, but unless the student does so it will be all the harder for him later to overcome his faulty pronunciation habits. "It is five or six times easier to establish the good pronunciation of a sound or word correctly than to break the habits of incorrect pronunciation."[5]

The first goal, then, in language teaching is to enable the

student to acquire a good pronunciation, and all efforts should be directed towards this goal. The students must acquire the habit of listening very closely to every nuance of pronunciation. It is not so important for them to pay close attention to the written letters as to the sounds they hear pronounced by their teacher. They must learn to imitate every feature of his pronunciation, even features which may seem a little strange to them. The teacher should say to his student: "Imitate what you hear, just as though you were a parrot or a phonograph record. Just listen and imitate." A student should count himself fortunate if his teacher has a good knowledge of phonetics. Such a teacher will be able to detect and correct mistakes in pronunciation; in many cases he will be able to prevent such mistakes.[6] The teacher should first illustrate a particular feature of pronunciation, then give his class an opportunity to repeat after him in unison, and finally listen to each of the students individually. Some teachers have only a part of the class (a row, etc.) repeat after them in unison, for a teacher trained in phonetics can very often detect pronunciation mistakes while listening to groups of ten or so. It is, however, impossible for him to do this while listening to an entire class.

Important as phonetic instruction is, it is equally important not to make the lesson monotonous and fatiguing by having excessively long phonetic drills. This danger is particularly present where the drill consists of isolated words. Drills of this sort are perhaps the most wide-spread, but they are linguistically unsound. The word is not the linguistic unit, but rather the sentence or the phrase. From the very first lesson the students should practice short sentences.[7] The rhythm and intonation of a sentence are as important as are the individual sounds. A person can learn to pronounce every word in a sentence correctly; but unless he has learned the proper sentence intonation and flow of language, people will recognize that he has a foreign accent the moment he begins to speak.[8]

The teacher of Hebrew does not have a very difficult task as far as pronunciation is concerned, if he himself pronounces correctly. The vowels are few in number and easy to pronounce; the consonants offer few difficulties (see the discussion further on). English speakers have very little difficulty in mastering Hebrew pronunciation. Their main problem is to develop a more energetic lip movement, for in Hebrew the vowels are stable and are not reduced, lengthened or diphthongized, as they are so often in English.

The Sephardic Pronunciation

The standard pronunciation of Hebrew in Israel is the Sephardic. It is the pronunciation one hears in the schools, in the theatre, on the radio; and it is the pronunciation that is steadily becoming the prevalent one in synagogues. The Ashkenazic Jews took the pronunciation over from the Sephardic Jews, and by doing so they felt that they were substituting the original form of Hebrew pronunciation for a form of pronunciation which had become corrupted in the Exile. Semitic scholars also considered the Sephardic pronunciation as the more correct form, judging from the transcriptions of Hebrew names in the Assyrian inscriptions, Greek transcriptions in the Septuagint and in Origen's Hexapla, the transcription of Greek and Latin words in the Talmud, and by comparison with Arabic which has best preserved the Semitic phonetic pattern.

However, the Sephardic pronunciation was not accepted in its entirety by the majority of speakers. In actuality, most Hebrew speakers continue to use the Polish-Russian form of Hebrew pronunciation and merely substitute *Patach* for *Kamatz* (i.e. the vowel *a* for *o*) and pronounce *undageshed tav* as *dageshed* (i.e. pronounce *t* instead of *s*),[9] and accent the last syllable rather than the syllable before the last. Apart from a few exceptions, the Ashkenazic Jews have not attempted to take over the Sephardic pronunciation of the *Chet* and *Ayin,* sounds which are so characteristic of Arabic pronunciation and the Hebrew pronunciation of those Jews who also speak Arabic, though there are "some Sephardic Jews as well who pronounce the *Ayin* like the *Aleph* and make no distinction between the two."[10]

Judging from the majority of Hebrew speakers in Israel, it can be said that in general the Ashkenazic Jews did not take over from the Sephardic Jews the pronunciation of the consonants but only the pronunciation of the vowels and the accentual pattern, and that the synthesis of the original Ashkenazic pronunciation and these particular Sephardic features constitute what we today call the "Sephardic" pronunciation.

The question of Hebrew pronunciation is no longer so heatedly debated as it was formerly. If we analyze current practice, we find that there are no differences of opinion in regard to the pronunciation of 21 of the phonemes indicated by the following 21 letters:

א — בּ — ב — ג — ד — ה — ז — י — פּ —

כ — ל — מ — נ — ס — פ — צ [11]

ר — שׁ (ימנית) — שׂ (שמאלית) — ת

As for the remaining five letters, some orthoepists wish to restore the original pronunciation of *Chet* and *Ayin*. While they are insistent upon this point, they tend to be less insistent in the matter of restoring the original pronunciation of the letters *Tet, Qof* and *Vav,* pronunciations heard today only from Arabic-speaking Jews.

Here and there one finds among the various Jewish communities advocates of a particular pronunciation of some of the other letters, but their influence is not very widespread. From the scientific point of view the pronunciation of the Yemenites is perhaps the most correct. The Yemenites not only differentiate between all the letters in the alphabet, but they even make a difference between *dageshed* and *non-dageshed Gimel, Dalet* and *Tav.*[12]

The Pronunciation of the Gutturals

There are those who insist on the use of the original pronunciation of the *Chet* and *Ayin* and maintain that it is impossible to revive Hebrew without reviving the original Semitic pronunciation. Due attention must be paid to the phonetic structure of a language. In the case of Hebrew, there should be a sound corresponding to every letter. In this way Hebrew writing would be completely phonetic and Hebrew spelling would offer no difficulty at all. Those who advocate the restoration of the "original" pronunciation of Hebrew feel that this task must be undertaken at the present moment when there is so large an influx of Arabic-speaking Jews. They urge that all teachers, particularly kindergarten teachers, learn the Hebrew pronunciation of the Arabic-speaking Jews, for there may never again be a similar opportunity for them to acquire and to teach the original form of Hebrew pronunciation.

However, there are many who oppose the restoration of the earlier pronunciation of the gutturals. Most writers, teachers, and public speakers are quite indifferent to the problem of distinguishing between the gutturals and make no attempt to differentiate *Aleph* from *Ayin* or *Chet* from *Chaf*. Very few of them attempt to argue the point; they merely ignore it. They feel that restoring the original pronunciation of the gutturals is not desirable, even if it were possible. They do not consider it necessary to imitate the guttural quality of Arabic; for them this is merely one of the traits of a desert dialect and not worthy of imitation on our part. We are now a Mediterranean nation and it is quite sufficient if our language takes on a Mediterranean coloring. There is no reason to expect a people which has become accustomed to the European languages to try to learn the pronunciation of sounds which were not pronounced even in Mishnaic times, and which have for the most part disappeared from all the Semitic languages with the exception of Arabic. If during the last fifty years we have not succeeded in restoring the original pronunciation of Hebrew, with the result that our high-school graduates do not distinguish between *Aleph* and *Ayin* or *Chet* and *Chaf*, how can we hope to succeed with the American and European Jews? It is far easier for the immigrants from Arabic-speaking countries, particularly for their children of school age, to give up their "guttural" pronunciation, than it is for the immigrants from Europe to acquire the difficult Semitic sounds. Moreover, it is visionary to suppose that Jews in Europe or America, among whom we wish to spread a knowledge of spoken Hebrew, will undertake to learn the proper pronunciation of the gutturals. Thus far, we have not even succeeded in having the Sephardic pronunciation adopted in all the Hebrew schools of the Diaspora.

As a matter of fact, our present problem with regard to the gutturals is not entirely new. The loss of certain of the gutturals is a very old phenomenon. We find it as far back as the Mishnaic period. The Rabbis of that period were often uncertain whether a given word was to be pronounced as if with an *Aleph* or an *Ayin*. We find quite a number of instances in the Talmud. Thus in the Tractate *Avoda Zara* (p. 2a) we find the question raised as to whether *"eydeyhen"* should be written with an *Aleph* or an *Ayin*. In *Erubin* (p. 7 a-b) the question is asked whether *"meabrin"* should be written with an *Aleph* or an *Ayin*. In the Tractate Shabbat we find the question raised several times: should *"garinin," "gemia," "omemot"* be written with an *Aleph* or an *Ayin*. We read criticisms of the Galilean pronunciation in which many of the gutturals were lost. When a Galilean pronounced the word אמר, people would mock him by saying: "Foolish Galilean! Do you mean חמור (donkey),

חמר (wine), or עמר (wool)?" Elsewhere (*Megillah*, p. 23b) we find that a priest who has any "defects" may not give the priestly benediction. In the Mishna and then in the Gemara it is explained that residents of Haifa or Bet Shan may not offer their benediction because they pronounce the *Aleph* like the *Ayin* and the *Ayin* like the *Aleph*. (Rashi remarks in his commentary that they would pronounce the word "*yaer*" in the Priestly Benediction with an *Ayin* instead of an *Aleph* and thus convert a word of blessing into its opposite.) Further on we read that "inhabitants of Bet Shan, Haifa and Tabun are not allowed to read the lesson from the Scripture in public because they confuse *Aleph* and *Ayin*."

As for the pronunciation of *Chet*, it should be observed that those who insist on the pharyngeal pronunciation of the *Chet* forget that in Biblical times there existed two types of *Chet*, a velar and a pharyngeal (exactly as in Arabic), even though only one letter was used in writing. Why, then, choose the pharyngeal pronunciation rather than the velar—the one in use today— when the latter is as original as the former. In fact, during the Mishnaic period the pharyngeal pronunciation of the *Chet* offered as much difficulty for many speakers as did the pronunciation of the *Ayin*. It is, for example, related of Rab Chiya that when he came to the verse "*vechikiti* (I waited) *la-adonai hamastir panav mi-bet yaakov*" (*Isaiah* 8), he seemed to say "*vehikiti*" (I struck), thus blaspheming the Lord's name (*Megillah*, 24b). Mistakes of this sort were principally found among the Galileans and among Jews of Babylonian origin, who were strongly influenced by Aramaic in which many of the gutturals had dropped out. But it is not only in Mishnaic Hebrew and in Aramaic that gutturals were lost; they disappeared even earlier in another important Semitic language, namely Assyrian. Four letters (corresponding to the Hebrew *Aleph*, *He*, *Chet*, and *Ayin*) were pronounced alike. This process in Assyrian was probably the result of contact with speakers of other languages which did not possess gutturals;[13] just as Hebrew speakers lost several of the gutturals when they were exiled among nations whose languages did not contain the Semitic gutturals.

We have spoken about the *Aleph* and *Ayin* and the *Chet* and *Chaf* at some length because those who have wished to restore the original Hebrew pronunciation have concentrated on these letters. They have not been as insistent on the restoration of the distinction between *Tet* and *Tav*, *Qof* and *Kaf*, or the bilabial pronunciation of *Vav* (i.e. like the English w). If none of the older values of these letters are restored, then Hebrew will have five pairs of letters in which both members of the pair are pronounced alike, namely, *Aleph-Ayin*, *Chaf-Chet*, *Tet-Tav*, *Kaf-Qof*, and *Vet-Vav*. This is not an altogether new phenomenon in our language. Our ancestors in Mishnaic times had the very same problems when they ceased to make a distinction between Samech and Sin and began writing words with Samech which appear in the Bible with Sin (e.g. תפש־תפס, שכין־סכין, חרש־חרס, שפק־ספק, כעש־כעס etc.[14] It is very possible that future generations may find it burdensome to have pairs of letters representing the same sound and may repeat the experiment we have just described in regard to the letter *Sin*. If our generation does not succeed in adjusting our speech to the written form of the language, coming generations may try to adjust the writing system to the pronunciation. A phonetic development of this sort can lead to many additional structural changes, for even the slightest phonetic readjustment may eventually lead to significant recasts in the entire morphological set-up of a language.[15]

The Problem of Gemination and the Vocal "Shva"

The pronunciation of the vowels also presents a problem. The strict orthoepists call attention to the fact that in the current pronunciation of Hebrew only a third of the vowels are pronounced. According to them a distinction should be made between long, short and "hurried" (i.e. half-long) vowels. But this distinction rests on a very complicated system of vocalization, and the attempt to introduce it into everyday speech has little prospect of success. On the other hand, Hebrew speech would be considerably improved if the practice of pronouncing geminated consonants and the *"shva"* were introduced. Except for the Yemenites and a few other small groups, Hebrew speakers disregard the *"strong dagesh"* (which appears in the written language to indicate a geminated consonant) and the *"vocal shva"* (which appears in the written language to mark the occurrence of the *shva* vowel—the vowel we have in the first syllable of the English word "belittle").

The *strong dagesh* is a very ancient feature of the language.[16] In general, it occurs where a consonant has been assimilated, as in נתנו instead of נתננו or אפל instead of אנפל ; it also indicates intensive action (*shibber* "he broke to pieces, smashed," as against *shavar* "he broke," *gannav* "one who is habitually given to stealing, a thief," as against *gonev* "one who steals, but is not an habitual thief"). Since the gemination of consonants has an important semantic function in the language, it is to be regretted that both Sephardic and Ashkenazic speakers neglect it.

Pronouncing the *"vocal shva"* would also help improve our current speech. In certain positions it is pronounced by most speakers of a word (e.g. *m'dina* "country, state," *t'chase* "you will cover," *b'ratson* 'gladly, etc." [17]) and in the middle of the word (e.g. *m'od'dim* "they encourage," *yishm'ru* "they will watch") but, on the whole, Hebrew speakers pay little attention to it. Here again we ought to make a serious effort to introduce this feature into our pronunciation.[18]

The introduction of these two features would not involve any great difficulty. Europeans and Americans do not find it hard to pronounce a geminated consonant or the *shva* vowel (the same cannot be said, of course, for the gutturals). Moreover, they are characteristic of most of the other Mediterranean languages, the chief features of which are, as compared with English, a greater proportion of vowels to consonants, and a more energetic pronunciation of the consonants, especially at the beginning and end of words.[19]

The Importance of a Unified Pronunciation

We have reviewed very briefly the principal problems involved in the improvement of Hebrew pronunciation. We have attempted to adopt a very moderate and realistic position because we believe that our principal objective should be to achieve a common standard pronunciation in Israel and in the Diaspora. Given the alternative of a "scientifically correct" pronunciation (the validity of which is questionable in a number of cases) and a unified one, we have naturally preferred the latter.

Jespersen [20] has defined a standard pronunciation as one which does not reveal the speaker's district of origin. The most important characteristic of the standard dialect is that the speakers cannot be identified as coming from particular regions; it provides a common medium of communication for people coming from different sections, each of which has its own local dialect. Local patriotism is often so strong that speakers will prefer their own regional dialect to the standard one, but such speakers usually prefer the standard dialect to that of regions other than their own.

There are those who deplore the spread of standard dialects because they mean the loss of local dialects with all their picturesqueness and vigor. However we must recognize that linguistic development in recent times has been away from local dialects. Today we prefer individual variations to regional variations. Among primitive peoples we find great regional variety — practically every tribe has its own dialect — but few speech differences between individuals. In contrast we find among civilized peoples relatively little regional differentiation (one has only to compare, for example, regions in central Africa where one may have a different language every hundred miles with the homogeneity of speech over the vast territory of the United States); but we do find a great deal of individual variation, even among speakers in one locality.[21]

The differences among the six Palestinian Arabic dialects (those spoken in Jerusalem, Nablus, Hebron, Gaza and those used by the Fellahin and the Bedouin), are at least as great— and probably even greater—than the forms of English spoken in cities as far removed as London, Edinburgh, Johannesburg, Sydney, Toronto and San Francisco. The differences in the Arabic spoken in Iraq, Egypt and Morocco are so great that a speaker from one country cannot understand or understands only with difficulty speakers coming from another. Language serves as a means of uniting groups, but it can also at times serve to separate them, as in the case of the Arabic-speaking countries where there are three forms of language (classical, mixed, and colloquial) or in India, where there are also three forms (Sanskrit, Prakrit, and Hindustani). Linguistic unification not only serves as a means of national and social unification, but is also a means of spreading the influence of a language, both in its spoken and its written form. It helps break down barriers of communication and enables a language to be understood over a wide area. But linguistic unification is possible only if there is a standard pronunciation; indeed "unless there is a standard pronunciation we have dialects but not a language."[22]

The Basis for a Standard Sephardic
Pronunciation Already Exists

What is the nature of the prevalent pronunciation in Israel?
We have already seen that the "Sephardic" pronunciation is not
Sephardic in the true sense. It has, to be sure, many Sephardic
elements, but they have been combined with other elements as
well. What pronunciation, in addition to the Sephardic, has
the greatest influence on present-day Hebrew speech? We can
answer negatively by saying that it is not the pronunciation of
immigrants from Germany, England, or Russia; nor of those
from Yemen, North Africa, or the Jewish communities of the
Near East. It is more difficult to give a positive answer. It seems
that the immigrants from Poland had a very great influence
in shaping current Hebrew speech because they formed the
majority of the immigrants that came during the period between
the two wars. In addition, for geographical or other reasons
the inhabitants of Poland seem to possess more adaptability to
foreign languages than inhabitants of other regions. Whenever
I have tried asking a class or any other group what form of
Hebrew pronunciation they perferred in general, or what form
seemed to them the best next to their own, the large majority
named the pronunciation used by the graduates of the schools in
Israel, or else the pronunciation of those speakers who came from
Poland. It is interesting to note that whereas members of the
oriental communities, particularly the older people, give prefer-
ence to the pronunciation of their particular communities, the
immigrants from Europe consider the accepted Israeli pronunciation as the best.

The emergence of a unified Hebrew pronunciation is taking
place at a very rapid rate. The large numbers of Jews who have
come to Israel recently have had their difficulties in learning
Hebrew, but they had no problem with the pronunciation as
such. The country is small and there are excellent means of
transportation, so that all parts of the country are in close contact. According to the census of November, 1948, 72 percent
of the Jewish population was concentrated in three large cities:
Tel Aviv, Jerusalem, and Haifa. In Israel, as elsewhere, the large
cities tend to develop a uniform pronunciation and set the pattern for the rest of the country. The rural population, which in
other countries tends to develop numerous local dialects, forms
one of the most educated groups in Israel, one of the bastions of

Hebrew language and culture. The differences in pronunciation in Israel are even smaller today than they were before the first World War, when the population was very small, the means of transportation poor, and contact between various parts of the country meager.[23]

We have today the basis for a standard pronunciation, even though a number of improvements are still necessary. This pronunciation does not give the older values to *Chet, Ayin, Tet, Qof,* and *Vav,* and even those who wish to restore the original pronunciation of the first two consonants rarely insist on the restoration of the last three.

One Hebrew expert on pronunciation has stated that a standard pronunciation has three purposes: to protect the individual from ridicule, to strengthen national unity, and to raise the cultural level by providing a model form of a language for people to use.[24] It is obvious that a form of pronunciation which imitates the Arabic does not satisfy the first two criteria. We are left, then, with the third criterion, that of the esthetic quality of our speech. Here the most important step would be to introduce geminated consonants and the *shva,* and to eradicate the literal translations of foreign expressions and idioms which are so widespread today, especially in the speech of the recent immigrants and their children.

Pronunciation Faults in the Various Groups

There are certain faults of pronunciation which require our immediate attention. These faults are most widespread in the first generation of immigrants and less so in the second and third generations. The most typical faults are:

1. The use of the sound *h* or *y* wherever *Aleph* or *Ayin* appears in the spelling; (*Ester* becomes *Hester; shomea* becomes *shomeya*). This is heard chiefly among immigrants from the Ukraine or from Turkey.

2. The unvoicing of *b, d, g, z.* This is heard chiefly from immigrants from Central Europe, who pronounce these sounds as *p, t, k, s.*

3. "H" is pronounced for "ch" (*achot* "sister" is pronounced *ahot; ma shlomcha* "how are you?" is pronounced *ma shlomha*). This pronunciation is especially heard among immigrants from Hungary, Czechoslovakia and Poland; and also among those from English-speaking countries.

4. The use of "dark l" (as in English or the Slavic languages) in place of a "clear l."

5. The use of "uvular r" (under the influence of Yiddish, French, etc.) instead of a "front r"; and among Americans the use of a palatal r.

There are also a number of common faults in the pronunciation of the vowels. We have already mentioned the fact that English speakers tend to lengthen the vowels, to introduce a glide element or even to dipthongize them. Russian speakers pronounce the *Cholam* like the *"aw"* sound in Russian, that is, a very open vowel halfway between the Hebrew *Patach* (*a*) and *Cholom* (*o*). Sephardic speakers do not pronounce the *Tsere*. Many Hebrew speakers—even native Israelis—pronounce the *Kamats Katan* (*o*) like the *Patach* (*a*) (e.g. *amnam* instead of *omnam*).

Another common fault is the accenting of the syllable before the last instead of the last,[25] especially in terms of endearment (*ábba* "dad," *sávta* "grandmother," *búbba* "doll"), in first names[26] and place names (*chánna*, "Anna," *yítschak* "Isaac," *rechóvot* "Rehovot"), in the second person plural of the past tense, and in a number of other words.

There is general agreement among all the Hebrew speaking communities that the misplacing of the accent is a fault that deserves our immediate attention.[27]

The Spread of the Sephardic Pronunciation

Of considerable concern at present is the matter of the Hebrew pronunciation used in the various countries of the Diaspora, particularly in that great center of Jewish life, the United States. The Sephardic pronunciation has made relatively little headway in the Hebrew schools of those countries. Unless there is a change in the situation we face the prospect of two forms of Hebrew pronunciation: the form used in Israel, and the form— or more correctly, the forms—used in the various countries of the Diaspora. Hebrew speakers in Israel may find difficulty in understanding the Hebrew spoken by their fellow Jews in the Diaspora and vice versa. Diaspora Hebrew may come to be regarded as an inferior form. The slow progress that has been made in introducing the Israeli pronunciation is attributable in large measure to the fact that synagogue services are almost uniformly conducted in the Ashkenazic pronunciation and to the fact that the teachers of Hebrew are not generally proficient in the Israeli pronunciation. The first factor has had a great influence; the sound of the prayers is extremely important for Jews accustomed to praying in the traditional pronunciation, particularly since many of them do not understand the content of the prayers. One finds a similar situation in the Catholic church where the service is conducted in Latin, in the mosques of India where the service is conducted in Arabic, and in the Buddhist temples of China and Japan where it is conducted in Sanskrit.[28]

In all these instances, the language used in the service is not understood by the masses, but is used because of the reverence in which it is held, and because it is a means of uniting all believers, whatever their native language.

The importance of unified Hebrew pronunciation in all synagogues and schools should not be overlooked. A common pronunciation can do much to create close unity among Jews in all parts of the world. Hebrew schools, teacher-training institutes and rabbinical seminaries should do everything in their power to introduce the Israeli pronunciation so that Jews in the Diaspora can share the same language. No time should be lost because, though it is easy enough to learn the Sephardic pronunciation at the beginning, it is difficult to acquire it after one has learned another pronunciation, for a great deal of effort has to be spent in unlearning the old habits before the new ones can be established. The change to the Sephardic pronunciation does not represent an insurmountable task. The teacher who possesses the necessary determination and persistence will have little difficulty.

Records, Films and Problems of Transcription

Teachers who are not entirely certain about their Hebrew pronunciation can make use of records which give the current Israeli pronunciation. The students, too, can in this way have an opportunity to listen to Hebrew correctly pronounced and carefully enunciated. Records possess the advantage that the student can listen to them whenever and as frequently as he desires. Even recent immigrants to Israel can derive great benefit from records and recording devices like Dictaphone and tape and wire recorders. Songs can also be of value in developing good pronunciation. Records of Israeli songs are popular in many countries, but unfortunately they are as often as not sung by people who know only a little Hebrew. Songs can be a very effective way of teaching Hebrew in general and Hebrew pronunciation in particular.

The best way to learn the pronunciation of a foreign language is, of course, through the imitation of native speakers or through listening to records or movies in the language. When it comes to learning pronunciation there can be no comparison between reading phonetic symbols and hearing the sounds pronounced, but phonetic transcriptions are useful, especially with the better students, if there is no, or little, opportunity to hear the spoken language.

Very important advances have been made in the field of phonetics in recent years. There is a system of transcription, that of the International Phonetic Association (known as the IPA), which is universally accepted and which has been used to transcribe the most diverse languages. Each basic sound (or "phoneme") is represented by a separate symbol. This phonetic alphabet is made up of the Latin letters, some of them with slight modifications; in a few cases arbitrary symbols are used. For most languages only a very small number of these arbitrary symbols—at most a dozen or so [29]—need to be added to the regular Latin letters in order to indicate the pronunciation of the language. In the case of a language which is written phonetically (e.g. Spanish, Czech, Finnish and Hungarian), there is, of course, no need for such a transcription system.

Since Hebrew writing is not completely phonetic, it is helpful to teach the students some transcription method. It must be recognized, however, that only older students, or those who have an aptitude for languages, take readily to phonetic transcription. For most students, a transcription system which has even a few strange symbols proves a stumbling block, since in every fourth word or so they will meet an unfamiliar symbol. The value of the transcription system is in direct relation to its accuracy and simplicity. For the more capable students, the IPA transcription is the best, since it is both accurate and simple. Experience has shown, however, that it is better not to use it with the majority of students, since "we all know the hostile reactions of students when they are confronted with phonetic transcriptions."[30] As a matter of fact, the language textbooks prepared by the American and British Armed Services use the ordinary English alphabet rather than the IPA symbols, despite the fact that the latter transcription method is more accurate.

We have to adopt a similar course in our Hebrew textbooks. In books intended for wide distribution, simplicity is more important than accuracy. In reality, complete accuracy is unattainable except where the student can listen to a teacher who has a good pronunciation or else to records which reproduce the standard pronunciation. Phonetic symbols can only provide rough indications of the pronunciation. Practice in imitating a teacher or records is the best way to acquire a good pronunciation.

NOTES ON CHAPTER THREE

1. Duff, *op. cit.*, p. 52.

2. Hayakawa, S. I., *Language in Action* (1947), p. 61f.

3. Handschin, *op. cit., p.* 179.

4. Fries, C. C., *Teaching and Learning English as a Foreign Language* (1945), p. 5.

5. Handschin, C. H., *op. cit.*, p. 288.

6. Barrows, S. T. and Cordts, A. D., *The Teacher's Book of Phonetics* (1926), p. 116f.

7. Jespersen, C., *Mankind, Nation and Individual* (1946), p. 86.

8. Barrows and Cordts, *op cit.*, p. 118.

9. Cp. Segal, M. S., *Foundations of Hebrew Phonetics* (1928) (in Hebrew).

10. Yellin, D., *Hebrew Grammar* (1942), p. 23 (in Hebrew).

11. The letter *Tsade* is pronounced by Arabic-speaking Jews as in the Arabic, but the consensus is that it is better to pronounce it as the Ashkenazic Jews do (i.e., as *ts*), since in this way Hebrew gains another phoneme found in many European languages, and, on the other hand, avoids adding another sibilant similar to *Samech and Sin.*

12. Goitein, D. Sh., *The Teaching of Hebrew in Israel* (1947), p. 78 (in Hebrew).

13. Brockelmann, C., *Semitische Sprachwissenschaft* (1916), p. 26.

14. This tendency to pronounce *Samech* and *Sin* alike was stopped in mid-course, as it were, and only a few words have remained in which we have *Sin* for *Samech.* In a few cases one member of a word family shows the old spelling whereas other members have the new; thus the word *"sevah"* (*gray hair; old age*) is written with *Sin,* but the word *"sav"* (*grandfather*) is written with *Samech; "sechel"* (*intelligence*) is written with *Sin,* but the related word *"histakel"* (*he looked at, observed*) is written with *Samech.*

15. Sapir, *op. cit.*, p. 186.

16. Yellin, *op. cit.*, p. 117.

17. We indicate the *shva* here by means of the IPA symbol.

18. Goitein, *op. cit.*, pp. 96-100. The author gives a number of practical suggestions for learning to pronounce geminated consonants and the *shva.*

63

19. *Ibid.*, p. 80.

20. Jespersen, *op. cit.*, p. 78.

21. *Ibid.*, p. 83.

22. Bialik, Ch. N., *"Machsorey Leshonenu Ve-Tikuna,"* *Dvarim Shebeal Pe* (1935).

23. For example, there was a local dialect in upper Galilee, particularly around Rosh Pinah, in which the *Vet* was pronounced *Bet*, e.g., מסתובבים הזבובים was pronounced with four *b's* instead of four *v's*. There also used to be more noticeable differences of intonation between workers, town dwellers, and members of the old Yishuv.

24. Goitein, *op. cit.*, p. 77.

25. Under the influence of those forms of the Ashkenazic pronunciation in which the syllable before the last is stressed. In the Sephardic pronunciation the accent is generally on the last syllable.

26. It is interesting to note that whereas more and more native speakers are beginning to accent men's names on the last syllable (*yitschák, yaakóv, gideón,* etc.) they still continue for the most part to accent women's names on the syllable before the last (*sára, rívka, dína, etc.*)

27. A classification of these mistakes is given in Booklet No. 61, published by the *Vaad Ha-Lashon Ha-Ivrit,* in the section entitled "Less Frequent Mistakes."

28. Hayakawa, *op. cit.*, p. 63.

29. Duff, *op. cit.*, p. 56.

30. Lind, *op. cit.*, p. 37.

CHAPTER FOUR

THE VOCABULARY OF ESSENTIAL HEBREW

The Investigation of Hebrew Word Frequencies

In teaching of a foreign language the problem of vocabulary
is most important. One who possesses a basic vocabulary can,
even if his knowledge of the grammar is limited, understand,
speak and read a foreign language in some measure. It is not
surprising therefore that those concerned with perfecting our
methods of foreign language teaching should from the very
first have devoted a great deal of their attention to determining
the best way of teaching vocabulary and more particularly of
deciding which should be the words taught.

During the last five or six decades more attention has been
paid to the problem of selecting and presenting the basic vocabulary than to any other problem.[1]

Indeed the advances made in this field were more rapid than
in any other aspect of language instruction. Though the achievements were of the highest importance they were unfortunately
not as widely utilized as they might have been. However, practice has lagged behind theory in such vital fields as hygiene,
public health, military strategy, to mention only a few.

Nevertheless the results achieved in the field of vocabulary
study have already had a very marked influence on foreign language textbooks, and "it seems certain that in time all elementary books and even advanced reading texts will employ the
vocabulary of these lists"[2] in order to determine what words
to introduce and in what order.

The first quantitative study of the vocabulary of a language
was made for German.[3] This was followed by a number of
important studies of the English vocabulary by Thorndike[4] and
Horne,[5] and of French, Spanish, Chinese, Hebrew[6] and Arabic.[7]
All these studies demonstrated the fact that a very limited number of words kept reappearing and thus formed the bulk of the
language. Thus Thorndike found that in English the ten most
frequent words make up 25 per cent of the written language,
the hundred most frequent words 59 per cent, and the thousand
most frequent words 90 per cent.

Similar results were obtained for Hebrew as can be seen from the following table:[8]

The Number of Most Frequent Words	Their Percentage Within the Running Vocabulary	
	In English Per Cent	In Hebrew Per Cent
10	25.0	12.0
50	50.0	30.0
100	58.8	41.0
500	82.1	72.3
1000	89.6	85.1
1500	93.2	91.7
2000	95.4	95.3
2500	96.8	
3000	97.7	
4000	98.7	
5000	99.2	
6000	99.5	

In order to determine the Hebrew frequency list some 200,000 running words were analyzed. These were found to be made up of 5,892 different words. Only 2,017 of them appeared 10 times or more.[8] The 2,017 words make up 95.3 per cent of the written language and the remaining 3,875 words make up 4.7

The count also revealed that the first ten words in the frequency list make up 12 per cent of the written language,[9] the first 100 words 41 per cent, the first 500 words 72 per cent, the first 1,000 words 85 per cent and the first 2,000 words 95.3 per cent.

These 2,017 words comprise accordingly the basic vocabulary of Hebrew. In teaching Hebrew we must first concentrate on this basic vocabulary. Only when the student has a thorough command of these words should we attempt to broaden his Hebrew vocabulary.

The first thousand words of the frequency list are for the most part general in nature. In the second thousand the vocabulary becomes more varied and the words included depend to an ever increasing extent on the nature of the material used. An analysis of three different frequency lists—those of Andersen,

Thorndike and Tidyman—in English[10] revealed that the first thousand words of all three lists were "very much alike." It was otherwise with regard to the second thousand: about 20 per cent (417 words) of Thorndike's first 2,000 were not among the first 2,000 words of either the Andersen or the Tidyman list. In the third thousand the wide divergence among the three lists seemed to indicate that over half of the words of any one list would be wasted on most pupils.

Comparative studies of frequency lists in other languages (French, German, Spanish, Hebrew, etc.) showed a similar situation: the first thousand words tend to be very similar in all the frequency lists prepared for language teaching (in most cases 70 per cent or more of the words are identical),[11] but beginning with the second thousand words the differences between the lists become greater and greater.

The 200,000 running words used for the Hebrew frequency count were taken from three main sources:

1) A third from private letters and from compositions written by 286 boys and girls
2) A third from private and business letters of 521 adults
3) A third from popular literary sources—the narrative portions of the Bible (to the extent of 60 per cent), representative selections from the Mishna (15 per cent), Agada (15 per cent) and the Prayerbook (10 per cent).

Modern Hebrew is not yet fixed in its forms as are English and French, for example. It is still undergoing very rapid change. Teachers and writers have a far greater influence on Hebrew than teachers and writers in Europe and America have upon their languages. Hebrew speech still draws to a very considerable extent from written sources. The language of the Bible, the Mishna and the Agada have had a great influence on Hebrew during the last 50 years and still exercise a marked influence on both spoken and written Hebrew. For this reason the Hebrew frequency list has been based upon these popular literary sources.

The present writer undertook three vocabulary counts: one based on the usage of children, one on the usage of adults, and one on popular literary sources. The three component counts together formed the Basic Word List of Everyday Hebrew. Words which frequently occurred in the popular literary sources but which did not appear in written Hebrew today were not included in the Basic Word List.

In order to indicate the degree of correspondence between these three lists we may give here the coefficients of correlation:

Rank Correlation Coefficients For Three Word Counts Compared With Each Other

Word Counts Compared	Correlation Coefficients	Probable Error
Children and Adults	0.982	+0.004
Children and Popular Literature	0.975	+0.005
Adults and Popular Literature	0.930	+0.013

The table above shows that the degree of correlation between the three component counts is very high.

The first 738 words in the Basic Word List of Everyday Hebrew may be considered as the rock-bottom vocabulary of the language. These 738 words have a frequency of 50 or higher,[12] and make up 80 per cent of the written language. The remaining words in the frequency list occur from 10-49 times in the 200,000 words counted. Since a frequency of 10-49 words is not adequate, we have reason to believe that if more running words were counted we might arrive at different results. Until a more extensive study is made we can continue to utilize the results of the existing count with the necessary reservations.[13]

An Attempt at a Basic Hebrew Vocabulary

As has already been explained, the frequency lists are compiled on the basis of written material. The lists do not therefore solve the problem of the spoken vocabulary. To be sure, the first several hundred words in the frequency list based on the written language are also for the most part the most frequent words in the spoken language, but past that number the differences begin to increase. Many words which are very common in the spoken language are relatively rare in the written language and vice versa.

Several attempts have been made to explore the frequency of words in the spoken language, the most important study being that made by the Bell Telephone Laboratories to tabulate the most frequent words in telephone conversations. The 79,390 running words counted were found to be made up of 2,240 words and their repetitions.[14]

Ogden has attempted in his Basic English to compile a list

of the most essential words of the spoken language. His list of 850 words (first published in 1929) was intended to provide the basic spoken and written vocabulary necessary for carrying on everyday affairs and for business and scientific purposes.[15] His primary purpose in devising his 850-word vocabulary was to make English an international language. People all over the world could readily master this small vocabulary and would thus have a means of communicating with speakers of other languages. In addition they would be able to read belles lettres and scientific literature written in Basic English. Important words of English and world literature were translated into Basic English. Daily broadcasts in Basic were instituted. The proponents of Basic English are convinced that it offers the easiest and quickest way of teaching standard English.

We need a "Basic Hebrew" to serve a similar purpose—that of providing "an international language" for the Jewish communities in the Diaspora. Just as the list of most frequent words can serve as a more efficient means of teaching reading, so the list of basic words can serve as the best means of teaching conversation. The two lists complement one another. The basic list contains words which do not have a high frequency in written material but which are very common in speech, and it differs from the frequency list in one very important respect. The frequency list gives the words which occur most frequently in the written material investigated, and the views of the investigator have no influence whatsoever on the order of the words in the list. The basic list on the other hand gives the words which are most vital for purposes of oral communication. The two lists naturally show a high degree of correspondence but there are many important differences between them. The basic list by its very nature cannot be as objective as the frequency list. The subjective judgments of the individual investigator are bound to play a role in determining the words selected. The frequency list and the basic list differ in the following respects:

1) The basic list does not include synonyms, even if they have a high frequency. We may cite here some examples from the first two Hebrew letters. In the frequency list we find several words for "but" (אך, אבל, אולם) ; in the basic list, however, we have only one (אבל). In the frequency list we find two words for "Mr." (מר, אדון) but only one in the basic list (אדון). Similarly we find:

In the frequency list אולי ,אפשר but in the basic only אפשר

,,	,,	,,	,,	,,	אחרי, אחר	,,	,,	,,	,, אחרי
,,	,,	,,	,,	,,	אמר, הגיד	,,	,,	,,	,, אמר
,,	,,	,,	,,	,,	אנו, אנחנו	,,	,,	,,	,, אנו
,,	,,	,,	,,	,,	אני, אנכי	,,	,,	,,	,, אני
,,	,,	,,	,,	,,	אפילו, אף	,,	,,	,,	,, אפילו
,,	,,	,,	,,	,,	בודאי, בטח	,,	,,	,,	,, בודאי
,,	,,	,,	,,	,,	בכל זאת, אף־על־פי־כן	,,	,,	,,	,, בכל זאת

Thus we have 21 words listed in the frequency list under the first two letters of the alphabet but only 10 in the basic list, and the same holds true of the remaining letters of the alphabet.[16]

2) The words in the basic list are used in as broad a sense as possible and are often used to cover words closely related in meaning. Thus the word אדם includes most of the meanings of איש but not all of them, yet in the basic list only איש appears and does service for אדם as well. Similarly the following words are not included in the basic list and more general words are used in their place:

אגודה instead of which only					חברה is used		
אל, בלתי	,,	,,	,,	,,	לא	,,	,,
אלא, כי אם	,,	,,	,,	,,	רק	,,	,,
חקלאי	,,	,,	,,	,,	אפר	,,	,,
אמנם	,,	,,	,,	,,	באמת	,,	,,
על ידי, בידי	,,	,,	,,	,,	אצל	,,	,,
אדמה	,,	,,	,,	,,	ארץ	,,	,,
־ש	,,	,,	,,	,,	אשר	,,	,,
אתו	,,	,,	,,	,,	עמו	,,	,,
הגיע	,,	,,	,,	,,	בא	,,	,,
בגד	,,	,,	,,	,,	לבוש	,,	,,
בהקדם	,,	,,	,,	,,	מהר	,,	,,
חנות	,,	,,	,,	,,	בית־מסחר	,,	,,
בנות	,,	,,	,,	,,	בחורות ילדות	,,	,,
בערך	,,	,,	,,	,,	כמעט	,,	,,
בעבור, בעד, למען	,,	,,	,,	,,	בשביל	,,	,,
במשך, בקרב	,,	,,	,,	,,	בתוך	,,	,,

In this way 24 words are eliminated from the basic list, and if we apply the same principle to the words under the remaining letters of the alphabet we eliminate a very large number of words. For purposes of communication it is sufficient if the learner knows one term which can cover a number of words,[17] just as it is sufficient for him to know one word for a given concept and not all the synonyms.

3) The elimination of certain words often has to be done at the expense of idiomatic usage.[18] We may cite here examples from the first two letters of the Hebrew alphabet:

Instead of			only		is included
		אחר כך	only	אחר זה	is included
,,	,,	אי אפשר	,,	אין אפשר	,, ,,
,,	,,	לו	,,	אם	,, ,,
,,	,,	אשה נשאת לבעל	,,	אשה לוקחת בעל	,, ,,
,,	,,	מגישים בקשה	,,	פונים בבקשה	,, ,,
,,	,,	בתור	,,	כמו	,, ,,

4) Certain words are eliminated from the basic list because it is possible to substitute other commoner words for them.[19] So the basic list excludes אחר since it can be expressed by באופן מיוחד; ביחוד since it can be expressed by בא אחרי הזמן הקבוע; בקר since it can be expressed by הלך אצלו or היה בביתו.

5) In Basic Hebrew the grammar is simplified as far as possible. Thus in the frequency list we have to give difficult forms like אביו, אחיו, בתו, but in Basic Hebrew we use the simple forms: האב שלו, האח שלו, הבת שלו

6) The basic vocabulary does not give abbreviations, whereas the frequency list must give them if they happen to occur in the material on which the list is based. This leads, for example, to a saving of five forms in the first two letters of the alphabet (א״י, בב״ח, א״ב, ביה״ס, בע״מ) and a corresponding saving in the other letters.

7) The basic list, like the frequency list, helps the learner by focusing attention on the central meaning of each word. Ordinary dictionaries list several meanings for words like ברכה, בחינה, בהיר, אבות, אבד, but in the basic list only the most important meaning is given. Where it is necessary to give two meanings for a word, each meaning is listed separately, just as though we were dealing with two different words. Thus the word רוח is listed twice, first in the meaning "wind" and secondly in the meaning "spirit."

8) A given verb in English can have many meanings de-

pending on the preposition used with it (see Chapter I). Hebrew does not possess this feature but it possesses one which is not less important—it has a rather limited (as compared with the European languages) stock of "roots" which appear in a large number of derived words. Once a student knows the meaning of a root he can guess the meaning of new words he encounters which contain the root. Many examples of words having the same root can be found in the first two letters:

אחרי — אחרון; איש — אשה; אכל — אכל; בן — בת; בנה — בנין
— בית; בחר — בחור — בחורה — בחירות.

Another feature of Hebrew which aids the learner is the frequent use of compounds: thus the word בית "house" enters into compounds like: בית־חולים, בית־חרושת, בית־כנסת, בית־מסחר בית־ספר.

Basic English does not contain international words or the names of measures, numbers, days of the week o̓r the months. These cannot be omitted so easily in Hebrew since it does not make the extensive use of international wo̓rds that English does.

The Use of Cognates in the Teaching of Hebrew

The importance of making use of cognates in language instruction has long been recognized. Even before the introduction of frequency lists or lists of basic words, teachers of modern languages understood the importance of pointing out to their students cognate words and expressions. It was found that 40 to 50 per cent of the English vocabulary is cognate with words in French, German, Spanish and Italian, and that the English speaker approaching the study of Spanish, for example, can recognize some 750 Spanish words because their cognates are found in English. "The use of English cognates and identicals as a means of learning foreign words is perhaps our most valuable means for building vocabulary, especially if reading is the objective." [21]

We have not paid sufficient attention in the teaching of Hebrew to the existence of cognate words in the mother tongues of the learners.[22] Students of Hebrew whose mother tongue is Arabic are in the advantageous position of the English speaker studying Spanish. The numerous cognate words in Hebrew and Arabic should constantly be pointed out (for this reason it is important that those teaching Hebrew to Arabic speakers should know enough Arabic to call attention to the similarities between the two languages). What, however, can be done in the case of the immigrants who come from Europe or America or those who study Hebrew outside of Israel? We must utilize as far as possible the Hebrew words which made their way into Yiddish, into the vocabulary of religious observance or into the terminology of Zionism. The number of such words cannot compare with the number of cognates occurring in the European languages or the number of cognates in Hebrew and Arabic but it is far from being a negligible quantity. Of the 1029 words listed in the Vocabulary of Essential Hebrew, about 25 per cent are used in Yiddish, in religious observances or in other aspects of Jewish life and folklore.

Thus in the first two letters of the alphabet we find the following words which are used in Yiddish:

בן־אדם, אוהב ישראל, אוודאי, אורח, מאכל, אמת, אספה, אפילו, בשום
אופן, אפשר, בהמה, בחור, בחורטע, ביצים, בית־חולים, בעל־בית, בן־יחיד,
בנין, בעל מלאכה, בערך, בקשה, בשעת, בת־יחידה, בעלי־בתים.

The following Hebrew words are part of Jewish life and folklore:

זכות־אבות, אגודת־ישראל, מים אחרונים, אמונה, ארבע כוסות,
ארון הקודש, עם־הארץ, בעל שם טוב, בקור חולים, בני ברית, ברכה.
Similarly, there are a number of Hebrew words which would be known to anyone familiar with Zionism or with Israeli life and institutions: אביב from תל־אביב; האהל, name of an Israeli theater; ארץ from ארץ־ישראל; אחד העם from אחד; באר; ארץ־ישראל from the teacher; הבימה, name of an Israeli theater from באר שבע. The teacher should take full advantage of these possibilities of making the acquisition of a Hebrew vocabulary easier for the beginner.[23]

A Compound Vocabulary of Essential Hebrew

Thus far we have considered three classes of words: 1) the most frequent words, 2) the basic words, and 3) cognate words. Each class has its own importance in the teaching of a foreign language. We have attempted to incorporate them into a composite "Vocabulary of Essential Hebrew."

The composite Vocabulary of Essential Hebrew which we give here is composed then of three layers: 1) the basic words, 2) the most frequent words, and 3) cognates. In order to determine the essential words we selected those words which seemed basic for everyday purposes and compared the 807 basic words obtained in this way with the frequency list. We found that 517 of the basic words were already included among the 738 words having a frequency of 50 or over, 208 of the basic words were included among the words having a frequency of 10-49, and 82 of the basic words were included among the words having a frequency of less than 10. These 807 basic words comprise about 80 per cent of our Vocabulary of Essential Hebrew.

The remaining 222 words in the list are derived from various sources. The chief source is the group of words having a frequency of 50 or more which for one reason or another were not included in the Basic List. For example, we did not include in the Basic List a word of high frequency that happened to be synonymous with, or closely related in meaning to, another word already selected. The word הגיע, for instance, was not included because it is synonymous with בא; and yet we felt it necessary to include it in the Vocabulary of Essential Hebrew because of its high frequency. In the same way we did not include in the Basic List words which had a high frequency but which were merely stylistic variants of another word: we did not give בעבור, or בעד for instance, since their general meaning is covered by בשביל. However, since these words have a very high frequency they are included in the Vocabulary of Essential Hebrew. Literary words like מאת or הטיל were not included in the Basic List but since they are of high frequency they also are included in the Vocabulary. Abbreviations were not included in the Basic List even though they were of high frequency. In the Vocabulary of Essential Hebrew we included 5 of the 17 abbreviations having a high frequency.

Some 24 words were drawn from another source, namely the Hebrew words and expressions which would be known by Yiddish speakers or by those familiar with Jewish religious tradition, the Zionist movement or present-day life in Israel. As was pointed out previously, there are over 250 such words in the Vocabulary of Essential Hebrew, comprising approximately a fourth of the total number of words. We stressed above in our discussion of cognates the important role these words can play in making it easier for many students to build up their Hebrew a very high frequency. Among these 250 words there are 24, some are taken from Yiddish vocabulary, which would be known by so many students that we included them in the high frequency. They are:

‏ו(שכור, שונא, סוחר, משל, משוגע, מציאה, חוצפה, חן, דוקא, בעל־מלאכה)
some from ‏ (עם ארץ, עונג שבת, מזל טוב, עליה, כשר, כלה, חתן);
Jewish tradition, folkways, etc. and some from the Israeli milieu
‏ (עלית הנוער, לאומי, חלוץ, הגנה, ארגון, חסיד, דרך ארץ).

The Vocabulary of Essential Hebrew is made up then of the following constituent parts:

1) A Basic Word List (comprising 517 words of high, 213 of medium, and 77 of low frequency) .... 807 words

2) Words of high frequency, not included in the Basic Word List [24] .... 198 "

3) "Cognate" words from Yiddish, Jewish folkways and Israeli milieu .... 24 "

Total   1029 words

THE VOCABULARY

In the Vocabulary of Essential Hebrew, which we present here, every word has been marked with one of 5 letters (in brackets): (B1), (B2), (B3), (F), (C). The mark (B1) shows that the word is basic and of high frequency; (B2) basic and of medium frequency; (B3) basic and of low frequency; (F) of high frequency but not basic; (C) cognate with expressions in Yiddish, Jewish folklore or Israeli milieu. This arrangement in five categories makes it easy for the user to eliminate a given category if he wishes to do so. The cognate words are given in the Hebrew spelling.

"Cognates"	English Equivalent	C	F	B₃	B₂	B₁	Word	
	father					x	אָב	1
	he lost					x	אָבַד לְ...	2
זכות אבות	forefathers				x		אָבוֹת	3
תל אביב	spring					x	אָבִיב	4
	his father	x					אָבִיו	5
	but					x	אֲבָל	6
	stone					x	אֶבֶן	7
	dust				x		אָבָק	8
אגדת ישראל	association	x					אֲגֻדָּה	9
אדון עולם	Mr.					x	אָדוֹן	10
בן־אדם	human being	x					אָדָם	11
	red				x		אָדֹם	12
	earth	x					אֲדָמָה	13
אוהב ישראל	he loved					x	אָהַב	14

"Cognates"	English Equivalent	Category					Word
		C	F	B3	B2	B1	
אהבה	love					x	אַהֲבָה 15
"אהל" (התיאטרון)	tent					x	אֹהֶל 16
	or					x	אוֹ 17
	perhaps	x					אוּלַי 18
	however	x					אוּלָם 19
	air			x			אֲוִיר 20
	airplane		x				אֲוִירוֹן 21
	light					x	אוֹר 22
אורח	guest		x				אוֹרֵחַ 23
	him					x	אוֹתוֹ 24
	then					x	אָז 25
	ear					x	אֹזֶן 26
	brother					x	אָח 27
	one					x	אֶחָד 28
	sister					x	אָחוֹת 29
	his brother	x					אָחִיו 30
	another					x	אַחֵר 31
	after	x					אַחַר 32
	he was late	x					אַחַר 33
	responsible		x				אַחֲרַאי 34
מים אחרונים	last				x		אַחֲרוֹן 35
אחרי ככלות הכל	after				x		אַחֲרֵי 36
	after him	x					אַחֲרָיו 37
	afterwards	x					אַחַר כָּךְ 38
	one (f.)				x		אַחַת 39
אפשר	impossible	x					אִי אֶפְשָׁר 40

"Cognates"	English Equivalent	Category					Word
		C	F	B3	B2	B1	
	which					x	אֵיזֶה 41
	how					x	אֵיךְ 42
	there is not					x	אֵין 43
	where				x		אֵיפֹה 44
	man					x	אִישׁ 45
	but		x				אַךְ 46
מאכל	he ate					x	אָכַל 47
	food					x	אֹכֶל 48
	farmer					x	אִכָּר 49
	to					x	אֶל 50
	don't		x				אַל 51
	but		x				אֶלָּא 52
	these					x	אֵלֶּה 53
	God					x	אֱלֹהִים 54
	(a) thousand					x	אֶלֶף 55
	if					x	אִם 56
	mother					x	אֵם 57
	bath-tub		x				אַמְבַּטְיָה 58
	his mother		x				אִמּוֹ 59
אמונה	faith					x	אֱמוּנָה 60
	indeed		x				אָמְנָם 61
	he said					x	אָמַר 62
אמת	truth					x	אֱמֶת 63
	we					x	אָנוּ 64
	we		x				אֲנַחְנוּ 65
	I					x	אֲנִי 66

"Cognates"	English Equivalent	C	F	B3	B2	B1	Word
	ship					x	אֳנִיָּה 67
	I	x					אָנֹכִי 68
	people					x	אֲנָשִׁים 69
	he gathered	x					אָסַף 70
אספה	meeting					x	אֲסֵפָה 71
	nose		x				אַף 72
	even	x					אַף 73
אפילו	even					x	אֲפִילוּ 74
בשום אופן	manner					x	אֹפֶן 75
אפשר	perhaps					x	אֶפְשָׁר 76
	possibility	x					אֶפְשָׁרוּת 77
	finger				x		אֶצְבַּע 78
	nearby					x	אֵצֶל 79
ארבע כוסות	four (m.)					x	אַרְבָּעָה 80
	forty					x	אַרְבָּעִים 81
ארגון צבאי לאומי	organization	x					אִרְגּוּן 82
	chest, box				x		אַרְגָּז 83
ארון הקודש	cupboard				x		אָרוֹן 84
	rice		x				אֹרֶז 85
	meal				x		אֲרֻחָה 86
	breakfast		x				אֲרֻחַת־בֹּקֶר 87
	lunch		x				אֲרֻחַת־צָהֳרַיִם 88
	supper		x				אֲרֻחַת־עֶרֶב 89
	cloth		x				אָרִיג 90
	long				x		אָרֹךְ 91
עם הארץ	country					x	אֶרֶץ 92

"Cognates"	English Equivalent	Category					Word
		C	F	B₃	B₂	B₁	
ארץ ישראל	Palestine					x	אֶרֶץ־יִשְׂרָאֵל 93
	fire					x	אֵשׁ 94
	woman					x	אִשָּׁה 95
	that, which					x	אֲשֶׁר 96
	he acknowl-edged	x					אִשֵּׁר 97
	(particle denoting a definite object)					x	אֶת 98
	you (f.)					x	אַתְּ 99
	you (m.)					x	אַתָּה 100
	with him	x					אִתּוֹ 101
	you (pl. def. obj.)					x	אֶתְכֶם 102
	you (pl. m.)					x	אַתֶּם 103
	yesterday					x	אֶתְמוֹל 104
	he came					x	בָּא 105
	representative					x	בָּא־כֹּחַ 106
	he explained	x					בֵּאֵר 107
באר שבע	a well				x		בְּאֵר 108
	please				x		בְּבַקָשָׁה 109
	garment					x	בֶּגֶד 110
	in her					x	בָּהּ 111
	bright			x			בָּהִיר 112
בהמה	animal					x	בְּהֵמָה 113
	early	x					בְּהַקְדֵּם 114
	in him					x	בּוֹ 115

"Cognates"	English Equivalent	C	F	B3	B2	B1	Word	
אוודאי	certainly					x	בְּוַדַאי	116
	postage-stamp		x				בּוּל	117
בחור	a young man					x	בָּחוּר	118
בחור'טע	a young woman		x				בַּחוּרָה	119
	examination				x		בְּחִינָה	120
	elections				x		בְּחִירוֹת	121
	he chose					x	בָּחַר	122
	in the hands of	x					בְּיָדִי	123
	especially	x					בְּיִחוּד	124
התיאטרון „הבימה׳	platform				x		בִּימָה	125
	between					x	בֵּין	126
ביצים	egg				x		בֵּיצָה	127
בעל וית	house					x	בַּיִת	128
	his house	x					בֵּיתוֹ	129
בית חולים	hospital				x		בֵּית־חוֹלִים	130
	factory					x	בֵּית־חֲרֹשֶׁת	131
	synagogue				x		בֵּית־כְּנֶסֶת	132
מסחר	business firm				x		בֵּית־מִסְחָר	133
בית ספר	school					x	בֵּית־סֵפֶר	134
	he wept					x	בָּכָה	135
	nevertheless				x		בְּכָל־זֹאת	136
	generally					x	בִּכְלָל	137
	without					x	בְּלִי	138
	un-		x				בִּלְתִּי	139

"Cognates"	English Equivalent	Category					Word
		C	F	B₃	B₂	B₁	
	in course of	x					בְּמֶשֶׁךְ 140
בֶּן־יָחִיד	son					x	בֵּן 141
	he built					x	בָּנָה 142
	daughters	x					בָּנוֹת 143
בִּנְיָן	building					x	בִּנְיָן 144
	for	x					בַּעֲבוּר 145
	for	x					בְּעַד 146
בַּעַל שֵׁם טוֹב	husband					x	בַּעַל 147
בַּעַל־בַּיִת	landlord				x		בַּעַל־בַּיִת 148
בַּעַל־מְלָאכָה	artisan	x					בַּעַל־מְלָאכָה 149
בְּעֶרֶךְ	approximately	x					בְּעֶרֶךְ 150
	bottle		x				בַּקְבּוּק 151
	morning					x	בֹּקֶר 152
בִּקּוּר חוֹלִים	he visited	x					בִּקֵּר 153
	inside	x					בְּקֶרֶב 154
	he asked for					x	בִּקֵּשׁ 155
בַּקָּשָׁה	request					x	בַּקָּשָׁה 156
	clear					x	בָּרוּר 157
	iron		x				בַּרְזֶל 158
„בְּנֵי בְרִית"	alliance					x	בְּרִית 159
	he greeted					x	בֵּרֵךְ 160
בְּרָכָה	greetings					x	בְּרָכָה 161
	for					x	בִּשְׁבִיל 162
	he cooked		x				בִּשֵּׁל 163
בִּשְׁעַת	during		x				בִּשְׁעַת 164
	meat					x	בָּשָׂר 165

"Cognates"	English Equivalent	Category					Word
		C	F	B₃	B₂	B₁	
בת־יחידה	daughter					x	166 בַּת
	his daughter					x	167 בִּתּוֹ
	within					x	168 בְּתוֹךְ
	as	x					169 בְּתוֹר
בעלי בתים	houses					x	170 בָּתִּים
	high (m.)				x		171 גָּבֹהַּ
	border					x	172 גְּבוּל
גבּוֹר	hero	x					173 גִּבּוֹר
	cheese		x				174 גְּבִינָה
	lady					x	175 גְּבֶרֶת
	roof				x		176 גַּג
	troop	x					177 גְּדוּד
	big					x	178 גָּדוֹל
	growing				x		179 גָּדֵל
	size				x		180 גֹּדֶל
גלות	Diaspora				x		181 גּוֹלָה
גוף	body					x	182 גּוּף
	wheel				x		183 גַּלְגַּל
	also					x	184 גַּם
	also				x		185 גַּם כֵּן
	he finished					x	186 גָּמַר
גן עדן	garden					x	187 גַּן
גנב	thief			x			188 גַּנָּב
	match		x				189 גַּפְרוּר
	rain					x	190 גֶּשֶׁם
	bridge				x		191 גֶּשֶׁר

"Cognates"	English Equivalent	Category					Word
		C	F	B₃	B₂	B₁	
	thing					x	דָּבָר 192
איבערדבר'ן	he spoke					x	דִּבֵּר 193
	fish				x		דָּג 194
	flag				x		דָּגָל 195
	sample					x	דֻּגְמָא 196
דוקא	just so	x					דַּוְקָא 197
	he pushed		x				דָּחַף 198
דינו	enough					x	דַּי 199
דין וחשבון	report				x		דִּין וְחָשְׁבּוֹן 200
דירה	apartment					x	דִּירָה 201
	door				x		דָּלַת 202
	blood					x	דָּם 203
דעה	opinion	x					דֵּעָה 204
	he knocked		x				דָּפַק 205
	thin				x		דַּק 206
	minute	x					דַּקָּה 207
דרום	south				x		דָּרוֹם 208
	demand	x					דְּרִישָׁה 209
	way					x	דֶּרֶךְ 210
דרך ארץ	good manners	x					דֶּרֶךְ־אֶרֶץ 211
	he demanded	x					דָּרַשׁ 212
	he gave light	x					הֵאִיר 213
הבדלה במוצאי שבת	difference				x		הַבְדֵּל 214
הבטחה	promise	x					הַבְטָחָה 215
	he promised	x					הִבְטִיחַ 216
	he brought					x	הֵבִיא 217

"Cognates"	English Equivalent	Category					Word
		C	F	B₃	B₂	B₁	
	he looked		x				218 הִבִּיט
	he understood					x	219 הֵבִין
הגדה	he told		x				220 הִגִּיד
	he arrived		x				221 הִגִּיעַ
	he presented		x				222 הִגִּישׁ
הגנה	defense	x					223 הֲגָנָה
	those		x				224 הָהֵם
	he					x	225 הוּא
	he led		x				226 הוֹבִיל
	he announced		x				227 הוֹדִיעַ
	announce-ment		x				228 הוֹדָעָה
	he added		x				229 הוֹסִיף
הוצאה	expenditure					x	230 הוֹצָאָה
	he drew out					x	231 הוֹצִיא
	he brought down					x	232 הוֹרִיד
	parents		x				233 הוֹרִים
	opportunity					x	234 הִזְדַּמְּנוּת
	he reminded		x				235 הִזְכִּיר
	he invited					x	236 הִזְמִין
	invitation					x	237 הַזְמָנָה
	he gave back		x				238 הֶחֱזִיר
	he began		x				239 הֵחֵל
	he decided					x	240 הֶחֱלִיט
	decision					x	241 הַחְלָטָה
	he threw		x				242 הֵטִיל

"Cognates"	English Equivalent	Category					Word
		C	F	B₃	B₂	B₁	
	she					x	הִיא 243
	he was					x	הָיָה 244
מכה	he struck	x					הִכָּה 245
הכנה	he prepared	x					הֵכִין 246
	he recognized					x	הִכִּיר 247
הכנסה	he put in					x	הִכְנִיס 248
	isn't it?	x					הֲלֹא 249
	further					x	הָלְאָה 250
הלואה	loan				x		הַלְוָאָה 251
	he went					x	הָלַךְ 252
	they					x	הֵם 253
	check	x					הַמְחָאָה 254
המצאה	invention		x				הַמְצָאָה 255
	he delivered	x					הִמְצִיא 256
	here is					x	הִנֵּה 257
	hither	x					הֵנָּה 258
	here he is	x					הִנֵּהוּ 259
	management					x	הַנְהָלָה 260
	the above-mentioned	x					הַנַּ"ל 261
	here I am	x					הִנְנִי 262
	he explained		x				הִסְבִּיר 263
	he agreed					x	הִסְכִּים 264
הסכמה	consent					x	הַסְכָּמָה 265
	he managed	x					הִסְפִּיק 266
„הסתדרות"	organization					x	הִסְתַּדְּרוּת 267
	he transferred					x	הֶעֱבִיר 268

"Cognates"	English Equivalent	C	F	B3	B2	B1	Word
	copy					x	הַעְתָּקָה 269
	he interrupted					x	הִפְסִיק 270
	intermission				x		הַפְסָקָה 271
	difference	x					הָפְרַשׁ 272
צער	he was sorry	x					הִצְטַעֵר 273
	he saved	x					הִצִּיל 274
	he succeeded	x					הִצְלִיחַ 275
הצעה	proposal					x	הַצָּעָה 276
	mountain					x	הַר 277
	he showed	x					הֶרְאָה 278
	much					x	הַרְבֵּה 279
הרג'נען	he killed					x	הָרַג 280
	he felt					x	הִרְגִּישׁ 281
	indeed	x					הֲרֵי 282
	lecture		x				הַרְצָאָה 283
	he left	x					הִשְׁאִיר 284
	he gave back					x	הֵשִׁיב 285
	he attained	x					הִשִּׂיג 286
שתדלנות	he endeavored	x					הִשְׁתַּדֵּל 287
א שמש	he used		x				הִשְׁתַּמֵּשׁ 288
	he took part	x					הִשְׁתַּתֵּף 289
	he was suitable, fit	x					הִתְאִים 290
	he made an effort	x					הִתְאַמֵּץ 291

"Cognates"	English Equivalent	C	F	B₃	B₂	B₁	Word
	effort					x	292 הִתְאַמְּצוּת
מחויב	obligation		x				293 הִתְחַיְבוּת
	he began		x				294 הִתְחִיל
	start				x		295 הַתְחָלָה
	competition		x				296 הִתְחָרוּת
חשוב	he took into account		x				297 הִתְחַשֵּׁב
כבוד	he had the honor		x				298 הִתְכַּבֵּד
	he wondered					x	299 הִתְפַּלֵּא
	development			x			300 הִתְפַּתְּחוּת
	took place		x				301 הִתְקַיֵּם
	etc.		x				302 וְכוּ'
	discussion				x		303 וִכּוּחַ
"וַעַד לאומי"	committee					x	304 וַעַד
	commission					x	305 וַעֲדָה
	conference				x		306 וְעִידָה
	this (f.)					x	307 זֹאת
	fly		x				308 זְבוּב
	this (m.)					x	309 זֶה
	gold					x	310 זָהָב
	this (f.)	x					311 זוּ
	cheap				x		312 זוֹל
זכות	right					x	313 זְכוּת
זכרון	he remembered					x	314 זָכַר
זמן (סמסטר)	time					x	315 זְמָן

"Cognates"	English Equivalent	C	F	B₃	B₂	B₁	Word
זקן	old					x	316 זָקֵן
	he sowed				x		317 זָרַע
	composition	x					318 חִבּוּר
	lovable	x					319 חָבִיב
	parcel	x					320 חֲבִילָה
חבר	comrade (m.)					x	321 חָבֵר
חבר׳תורין	comrade (f.)					x	322 חֲבֵרָה
חברה	company					x	323 חָבְרָה
חגא	holiday	x					324 חַג
	celebration				x		325 חֲגִיגָה
	sharp		x				326 חַד
חדר (בית ספר)	room					x	327 חָדָר
חודש	month					x	328 חֹדֶשׁ
	new					x	329 חָדָשׁ
חוב	debt					x	330 חוֹב
	duty					x	331 חוֹבָה
	contract	x					332 חוֹזֶה
	thread			x			333 חוּט
בקור חולים	sick					x	334 חוֹלֶה
	coast			x			335 חוֹף
חוץ	except	x					336 חוּץ מ...
חוץ לארץ	outside					x	337 חוּץ
	hole			x			338 חוֹר
	strong					x	339 חָזָק
	be strong and of good courage	x					340 חֲזַק וֶאֱמַץ

"Cognates"	English Equivalent	Category					Word
		C	F	B3	B2	B1	
איבערחזר'ן	he came back	x					חָזַר 341
	alive				x		חַי 342
	owing	x					חָיָב 343
חיה	animal				x		חַיָה 344
	his life	x					חָיָיו 345
לחיים	life				x		חַיִּים 346
	he waited				x		חִכָּה 347
תלמיד חכם	wise				x		חָכָם 348
חכמה	wisdom			x			חָכְמָה 349
	milk				x		חָלָב 350
חלום	dream				x		חֲלוֹם 351
	window			x			חַלּוֹן 352
חלוץ	pioneer		x				חָלוּץ 353
חלק	part				x		חֵלֶק 354
	he distributed		x				חִלֵּק 355
	hot			x			חַם 356
	butter			x			חֶמְאָה 357
חמור	donkey				x		חֲמוֹר 358
	material				x		חֹמֶר 359
חמשה עשר	five (m.)				x		חֲמִשָּׁה 360
חן	charm	x					חֵן 361
	education			x			חִנּוּךְ 362
	shop			x			חֲנוּת 363
חסיד	a follower	x					חָסִיד 364
	missing				x		חָסַר 365

"Cognates"	English Equivalent	Category					Word
		C	F	B₃	B₂	B₁	
	he looked for	x					חִפֵּשׂ 366
	freedom					x	חֹפֶשׁ 367
	skirt			x			חֲצָאִית 368
	half					x	חֲצִי 369
חוצפה	impudence	x					חֻצְפָּה 370
	yard	x					חָצֵר 371
	agriculturist	x					חַקְלָאִי 372
	winter			x			חֹרֶף 373
	he ploughed			x			חָרַשׁ 374
	he thought					x	חָשַׁב 375
חשבון	account					x	חֶשְׁבּוֹן 376
חשוב	important			x			חָשׁוּב 377
	darkness			x			חֹשֶׁךְ 378
	cat		x				חָתוּל 379
חתונה	wedding		x				חֲתוּנָה 380
חתן	bridegroom	x					חָתָן 381
	he signed	x					חָתַם 382
טבע	nature			x			טֶבַע 383
יום־טוב	good					x	טוֹב 384
טובה	favor					x	טוֹבָה 385
	trip					x	טִיּוּל 386
	he took a walk	x					טִיֵּל 387
טעות	mistake					x	טָעוּת 388
טעם	taste			x			טַעַם 389
טענה	argument			x			טַעֲנָה 390

"Cognates"	English Equivalent	Category					Word	
		C	F	B₃	B₂	B₁		
	drop		x				טִפָּה	391
טפש	fool		x				טִפֵּשׁ	392
	fresh			x			טָרִי	393
	before	x					טֶרֶם	394
	he will eat					x	יֹאכַל	395
	he will say					x	יֹאמַר	396
	he will come					x	יָבוֹא	397
	dry			x			יָבֵשׁ	398
	hand					x	יָד	399
	known	x					יָדוּעַ	400
	friend	x					יְדִיד	401
ידיעה	knowledge					x	יְדִיעָה	402
	he knew					x	יָדַע	403
	he will know					x	יֵדַע	404
	Jew					x	יְהוּדִי	405
	let it be	x					יְהִי	406
	(it) he will be					x	יִהְיֶה	407
	will he kindly	x					יוֹאִיל	408
יום־טוב	day					x	יוֹם	409
	more					x	יוֹתֵר	410
	together					x	יַחַד	411
	wine				x		יַיִן	412
	he was able					x	יָכֹל	413
	ability	x					יְכֹלֶת	414
	little boy					x	יֶלֶד	415
	little girl					x	יַלְדָּה	416

"Cognates"	English Equivalent	Category					Word
		C	F	B₃	B₂	B₁	
	he will walk					x	יֵלֵךְ 417
	bag, knapsack				x		יַלְקוּט 418
יִם	sea					x	יָם 419
א מת	he will die	x					יָמוּת 420
ימים טובים	days					x	יָמִים 421
	right					x	יָמִין 422
	he will rest	x					יָנוּחַ 423
קרן היסוד	foundation					x	יְסוֹד 424
	he will drop in	x					יָסוּר 425
	he will travel					x	יִיסַע 426
	he will answer					x	יַעֲנֶה 427
	forest				x		יַעַר 428
	pretty					x	יָפֶה 429
	he went out					x	יָצָא 430
	he will get up					x	יָקוּם 431
	dear					x	יָקָר 432
	he will see					x	יִרְאֶה 433
	he went down					x	יָרַד 434
	he will run				x		יָרוּץ 435
	green				x		יָרֹק 436
	vegetables				x		יְרָקוֹת 437
	there is					x	יֵשׁ 438
	he sat					x	יָשַׁב 439
	he will sit					x	יֵשֵׁב 440

"Cognates"	English Equivalent	Category					Word
		C	F	B₃	B₂	B₁	
	he will return					x	יָשׁוּב 441
יֹשׁוּב	settlement				x		יִשּׁוּב 442
יְשִׁיבָה	session					x	יְשִׁיבָה 443
	direct	x					יָשִׁיר 444
	he slept				x		יָשֵׁן 445
	straight					x	יָשָׁר 446
יִשְׂרָאֵל	Israel					x	יִשְׂרָאֵל 447
	he will give					x	יִתֵּן 448
	remainder					x	יֶתֶר 449
	pain				x		כְּאֵב 450
	as if	x					כְּאָלוּ 451
	here					x	כָּאן 452
	when					x	כַּאֲשֶׁר 453
מכבד זיין	he honored					x	כִּבֵּד 454
	heavy					x	כָּבֵד 455
כָּבוֹד	his honor					x	כְּבוֹדוֹ 456
	highway			x			כְּבִישׁ 457
	laundry		x				כְּבִיסָה 458
	already					x	כְּבָר 459
	pitcher			x			כַּד 460
כְּדַאי	worthwhile				x		כְּדַאי 461
	in order to	x					כְּדִי 462
	ball				x		כַּדּוּר 463
כְּדִי	thus	x					כֹּה 464
	hat		x				כּוֹבַע 465
	star				x		כּוֹכָב 466

"Cognates"	English Equivalent	Category					Word
		C	F	B₃	B₂	B₁	
ארבע כוסות	glass, cup				x		467 כּוֹס
כוח	strength					x	468 פֹּחַ
	blue				x		469 כָּחֹל
	because					x	470 כִּי
	because	x					471 כֵּיוָן שֶׁ ...
	pocket				x		472 כִּיס
	so					x	473 כָּךְ
	so	x					474 כָּכָה
	all					x	475 כֹּל
	all of it (him)					x	476 כֻּלּוֹ
כלב	dog				x		477 כֶּלֶב
כלה	bride	x					478 כַּלָּה
כלים	tool					x	479 כְּלִי
	so much					x	480 כָּל־כָּךְ
כלל	general					x	481 כְּלָלִי
	how much, how many					x	482 כַּמָּה
	as, like					x	483 כְּמוֹ
	like him (it)					x	484 כָּמוֹהוּ
	quantity		x				485 כַּמּוּת
כמעט	almost					x	486 כִּמְעַט
	yes					x	487 כֵּן
	entrance					x	488 כְּנִיסָה
כנסת	Israel Parliament				x		489 כְּנֶסֶת
	chair					x	490 כִּסֵּא
	he covered	x					491 כִּסָּה

"Cognates"	English Equivalent	Category					Word	
		C	F	B₃	B₂	B₁		
כסף	money					x	כֶּסֶף	492
	at present	x					כָּעֵת	493
	palm					x	כַּף	494
	spoon		x				כַּף	495
	according to	x					כְּפִי	496
	village				x		כְּפָר	497
	ticket				x		כַּרְטִיס	498
	vineyard					x	כֶּרֶם	499
כשר	(ritually) fit food	x					כָּשֵׁר	500
לשנה טובה תכתבו	he wrote					x	כָּתַב	501
	address				x		כְּתֹבֶת	502
	writing	x					כְּתִיבָה	503
	shirt				x		כֻּתֹּנֶת	504
	no					x	לֹא	505
	slowly				x		לְאַט	506
ועד לאומי ארגון צבאי לאומי	national	x					לְאֻמִּי	507
	heart					x	לֵב	508
	he alone					x	לְבַדּוֹ	509
	his heart	x					לִבּוֹ	510
	white				x		לָבָן	511
לבנה	moon		x				לְבָנָה	512
	brick		x				לְבֵנָה	513
א מלבוש	he put on					x	לָבַשׁ	514
	completely	x					לְגַמְרִי	515
	to know					x	לָדַעַת	516

"Cognates"	English Equivalent	Category					Word
		C	F	B₃	B₂	B₁	
	to her					x	517 לָהּ
	to thank	x					518 לְהוֹדוֹת
	to be					x	519 לִהְיוֹת
	to them (m.)					x	520 לָהֶם
	good-bye, see you later			x			521 לְהִתְרָאוֹת
	to him					x	522 לוֹ
	blackboard			x			523 לוּחַ
לחם	bread					x	524 לֶחֶם
	Israeli pound	x					525 לִ״י
							(לִירָה יִשְׂרְאֵלִית)
	to me					x	526 לִי
	night					x	527 לַיְלָה
	to you (m.)					x	528 לְךָ
	go!					x	529 לַךְ
	to Mr., Mrs. or Miss (addressee)	x					530 לכ׳ (לִכְבוֹד)
	to you (pl. m.)					x	531 לָכֶם
	therefore	x					532 לָכֵן
	to walk					x	533 לָלֶכֶת
א למדן	he studied					x	534 לָמַד
מלמד	he taught					x	535 לִמֵּד
	why					x	536 לָמָּה
	study					x	537 לִמּוּד
	below					x	538 לְמַטָּה
	above					x	539 לְמַעְלָה

"Cognates"	English Equivalent	Category					Word
		C	F	B₃	B₂	B₁	
	for the sake of	x					540 לְמַעַן
	in advance [1]	x					541 לְמַפְרֵעַ
	to us					x	542 לָנוּ
לְעֵת עַתָּה	meanwhile			x			543 לְעֵת עַתָּה
	in accordance with	x					544 לְפִי
	before					x	545 לְפְנֵי
	before him					x	546 לְפָנָיו
	sometimes			x			547 לִפְעָמִים
	dessert		x				548 לִפְתָּן
	to go out					x	549 לָצֵאת
	he took					x	550 לָקַח
א לקחן	to take					x	551 לָקַחַת
	towards him	x					552 לִקְרָאתוֹ
	on the occasion of	x					553 לְרֶגֶל
	to return					x	554 לָשׁוּב
לָשׁוֹן	tongue			x			555 לָשׁוֹן
	to put					x	556 לָשִׂים
	chamber	x					557 לִשְׁכָּה
	for the purpose of	x					558 לְשֵׁם
	to give					x	559 לָתֵת
	very					x	560 מְאֹד
מֵאָה	hundred					x	561 מֵאָה

---

[1] This meaning, though incorrect, is commonly used.

"Cognates"	English Equivalent	Category					Word
		C	F	B3	B2	B1	
	by (an author)	x					562 מֵאֵת
	brush		x				563 מִבְרֶשֶׁת
מדבר	desert				x		564 מִדְבָּר
	measure				x		565 מִדָּה
	why	x					566 מַדּוּעַ
מדינה	state				x		567 מְדִינָה
	science				x		568 מַדָּע
	guide				x		569 מַדְרִיךְ
	what					x	570 מַה
	quick		x				571 מָהִיר
	from them (m.)					x	572 מֵהֶם
	quickly					x	573 מַהֵר
	(self) understood					x	574 מוּבָן
	ready			x			575 מוּכָן
	native country	x					576 מוֹלֶדֶת
	institution				x		577 מוֹסָד
	council	x					578 מוֹעֲצָה
	teacher (m.)				x		579 מוֹרֶה
	teacher (f.)		x				580 מוֹרָה
	colony				x		581 מוֹשָׁבָה
	death				x		582 מָוֶת
	suitcase		x				583 מִזְוָדָה
	secretary				x		584 מַזְכִּיר

"Cognates"	English Equivalent	Category					Word
		C	F	B₃	B₂	B₁	
מזל טוב	good luck	x					585 מַזָּל טוֹב
מזרח הסתדרות "מזרחי"	east				x		586 מִזְרָח
מוח	brain				x		587 מֹחַ
	copybook		x				588 מַחְבֶּרֶת
	needle		x				589 מַחַט
	price					x	590 מְחִיר
	disease					x	591 מַחֲלָה
	department					x	592 מַחְלָקָה
מחנה	camp				x		593 מַחֲנֶה
	storeroom					x	594 מַחְסָן
	tomorrow					x	595 מָחָר
	a thought				x		596 מַחֲשָׁבָה
	kitchen					x	597 מִטְבָּח
	bed					x	598 מִטָּה
	umbrella		x				599 מִטְרִיָּה
	who					x	600 מִי
	special				x		601 מְיוּחָד
מים אחרונים	water					x	602 מַיִם
א מִין	kind					x	603 מִין
מכות	blow				x		604 מַכָּה
	machine					x	605 מְכוֹנָה
	car		x				606 מְכוֹנִית
	from you (pl. m.)					x	607 מִכֶּם
	trousers		x				608 מִכְנָסַיִם

"Cognates"	English Equivalent	Category					Word	
		C	F	B₃	B₂	B₁		
	he sold					x	מָכַר	609
	letter					x	מִכְתָּב	610
	full					x	מָלֵא	611
	he filled	x					מִלֵּא	612
	word				x		מִלָּה	613
	hotel				x		מָלוֹן	614
	salt				x		מֶלַח	615
מלחמה	war					x	מִלְחָמָה	616
מלך	king					x	מֶלֶךְ	617
מלכה	queen				x		מַלְכָּה	618
	from him					x	מִמֶּנּוּ	619
	government					x	מֶמְשָׁלָה	620
	from					x	מִן	621
	manager					x	מְנַהֵל	622
מנוחה	rest					x	מְנוּחָה	623
	tax					x	מַס	624
מסחר	commerce			x			מִסְחָר	625
	nail	x					מַסְמֵר	626
	number					x	מִסְפָּר	627
	scissors	x					מִסְפָּרַיִם	628
מסר'ן	he delivered					x	מָסַר	629
	comb	x					מַסְרֵק	630
	little					x	מְעַט	631
	envelope	x					מַעֲטָפָה	632
	coat	x					מְעִיל	633
	interesting			x			מְעַנְיֵן	634

"Cognates"	English Equivalent	C	F	B₃	B₂	B₁	Word
מערב	west		x				635 מַעֲרָב
	deed					x	636 מַעֲשָׂה
	party				x		637 מִפְלַגָּה
	because					x	638 מִפְּנֵי
	key		x				639 מַפְתֵּחַ
מציאה	he found					x	640 מָצָא
	state, situation					x	641 מַצָּב
מציאה	bargain	x					642 מְצִיאָה
	place					x	643 מָקוֹם
	stick				x		644 מַקֵּל
	showerbath		x				645 מִקְלַחַת
	shelter		x				646 מִקְלָט
	accident					x	647 מִקְרֶה
	refrigerator		x				648 מְקָרֵר
	bitter				x		649 מַר
	Mr.	x					650 מַר
	center					x	651 מֶרְכָּז
	soup		x				652 מָרָק
	pump				x		653 מַשְׁאֵבָה
משוגע	mad	x					654 מְשֻׁגָּע
	game				x		655 מִשְׂחָק
	tooth-paste		x				656 מִשְׁחַת־שִׁנַּיִם
	police				x		657 מִשְׁטָרָה
	silk		x				658 מֶשִׁי
	he pulled				x		659 מָשַׁךְ
משל	example	x					660 מָשָׁל

"Cognates"	English Equivalent	Category					Word
		C	F	B₃	B₂	B₁	
משלוח מנות	delivery	x					מִשְׁלוֹחַ 661
משפחה	family					x	מִשְׁפָּחָה 662
זיך משפט'ן	judgment					x	מִשְׁפָּט 663
	small farm					x	מָשָׁק 664
	weight					x	מִשְׁקָל 665
	office					x	מִשְׂרָד 666
א מת	he died					x	מֵת 667
	from within	x					מִתּוֹךְ 668
	sweet				x		מָתוֹק 669
	when					x	מָתַי 670
	metal		x				מַתֶּכֶת 671
מתנה	gift				x		מַתָּנָה 672
	please	x					נָא 673
	faithful					x	נֶאֱמָן 674
	it was said					x	נֶאֱמַר 675
נביא	prophet					x	נָבִיא 676
מתנגד	opposite					x	נֶגֶד 677
מנהג	he drove	x					נָהַג 678
	driver		x				נֶהָג 679
	he managed					x	נִהֵל 680
	comfortable				x		נוֹחַ 681
	he was born	x					נוֹלַד 682
ימים נוראים	terrible				x		נוֹרָא 683
	necessary					x	נָחוּץ 684
	stream				x		נַחַל 685
	charming				x		נֶחְמָד 686

"Cognates"	English Equivalent	Category					Word
		C	F	B₃	B₂	B₁	
	snake				x		נָחָשׁ 687
	he was inclined	x					נָטָה 688
	paper			x			נְיָר 689
	right					x	נָכוֹן 690
	he entered					x	נִכְנַס 691
מלחמה	he fought					x	נִלְחַם 692
	low			x			נָמוּךְ 693
	harbor			x			נָמֵל 694
	he was found					x	נִמְצָא 695
בעל נסיון	experience			x			נִסָּיוֹן 696
נסיעה	voyage					x·	נְסִיעָה 697
	he traveled					x	נָסַע 698
	pleasant					x	נָעִים 699
	shoe			x			נַעַל 700
	boy					x	נַעַר 701
	he fell					x	נָפַל 702
	soul					x	נֶפֶשׁ 703
	point			x			נְקוּדָה 704
	clean			x			נָקִי 705
	he carried					x	נָשָׂא 706
	he remained					x	נִשְׁאַר 707
שבועה	he swore	x					נִשְׁבַּע 708
	president			x			נָשִׂיא 709
	bite (n.)		x				נְשִׁיכָה 710
נשים	women					x	נָשִׁים 711

"Cognates"	English Equivalent	C	F	B3	B2	B1	Word	
	kiss (n.)			x			נְשִׁיקָה	712
	it was heard					x	נִשְׁמַע	713
	evening party soirée	x					נָשָׁף	714
	he was summoned	x					נִתְבַּע	715
	he gave					x	נָתַן	716
	cause					x	סִבָּה	717
	soap				x		סַבּוֹן	718
	around					x	סָבִיב	719
	environment					x	סְבִיבָה	720
	porter		x				סַבָּל	721
	he closed					x	סָגַר	722
	he arranged					x	סָדַר	723
סדר של פסח	order					x	סָדָר	724
סוֹחֵר	businessman	x					סוֹחֵר	725
	horse					x	סוּס	726
סוּף	end					x	סוֹף	727
סחורה	goods					x	סְחוֹרָה	728
סך הכל	sum	x					סָךְ	729
	pin		x				סִכָּה	730
	account	x					סְכוּם	731
	knife				x		סַכִּין	732
סכנה	danger				x		סַכָּנָה	733
	sugar		x				סֻכָּר	734
	basket		x				סַל	735
	he forgave	x					סָלַח	736

"Cognates"	English Equivalent	Category					Word
		C	F	B₃	B₂	B₁	
סליחות (בבית הכנסת)	pardon		x				סְלִיחָה 737
	he settled (an account)	x					סִלֵּק 738
	shoemaker		x				סַנְדְּלָר 739
	branch	x					סְנִיף 740
	story			x			סִפּוּר 741
	he told					x	סִפֵּר 742
ספר תורה	book					x	סֵפֶר 743
	he worked					x	עָבַד 744
	his slave	x					עַבְדוֹ 745
	thick			x			עָבָה 746
עבודה זרה	work					x	עֲבוֹדָה 747
	he passed					x	עָבַר 748
	Hebrew					x	עִבְרִית 749
	cake		x				עֻגָּה 750
	circle		x				עָגוּל 751
	till					x	עַד 752
	witness	x					עֵד 753
	still	x					עֲדַיִן 754
	worker					x	עוֹבֵד 755
	still					x	עוֹד 756
(אַ גרויסער) עולם	world					x	עוֹלָם 757
עוף	poultry			x			עוֹף 758
	he left					x	עָזַב 759
	he helped	x					עָזַר 760
	help					x	עֶזְרָה 761

"Cognates"	English Equivalent	Category					Word
		C	F	B₃	B₂	B₁	
	pen		x				עֵט 762
בלי עין הרע	eye					x	עַיִן 763
	tired				x		עָיֵף 764
	town					x	עִיר 765
	now					x	עַכְשָׁו 766
	upon					x	עַל 767
	beside		x				עַל־יַד 768
	by					x	עַל־יְדֵי 769
	he went up					x	עָלָה 770
עלית הנוער	immigration to Israel	x					עָלִיָה 771
עלית הנוער	immigration of youth to Israel	x					עָלִיַת־נֹעַר 772
	on him					x	עָלָיו 773
עם ארץ	a people					x	עַם 774
עם הארץ	an ignorant fellow	x					עַם־הָאָרֶץ 775
	with					x	עִם 776
	he stood					x	עָמַד 777
	page		x				עַמּוּד 778
„עמק" (יזרעאל)	valley				x		עֵמֶק 779
	deep				x		עָמֹק 780
„עונג שבת", תענוג	pleasure	x					עֹנֶג 781
	he answered					x	עָנָה 782
	poor				x		עָנִי 783
עניין	matter		x				עִנְיָן 784

"Cognates"	English Equivalent	C	F	B3	B2	B1	Word
עסק	business				x		785 עֵסֶק
	pencil		x				786 עִפָּרוֹן
	wood					x	787 עֵץ
	himself (itself)					x	788 עַצְמוֹ (בְּעַצְמוֹ)
ערב שבת	evening					x	789 עֶרֶב
	Arab					x	790 עֲרָבִי
	towns	x					791 עָרִים
„שלחן ערוך"	he arranged	x					792 עָרַךְ
בערך	value					x	793 עֵרֶךְ
	grass				x		794 עֵשֶׂב
	he made					x	795 עָשָׂה
ינעשר	rich				x		796 עָשִׁיר
	he smoked		x				797 עָשַׁן
עשרה בטבת	ten (m.)					x	798 עֲשָׂרָה
	twenty					x	799 עֶשְׂרִים
מעת לעת	time	x					800 עֵת
לעת עתה	now	x					801 עַתָּה
	newspaper					x	802 עִתּוֹן
	future				x		803 עָתִיד
	meeting		x				804 פְּגִישָׁה
	he met	x					805 פָּגַשׁ
	mouth				x		806 פֶּה
	here	x					807 פֹּה
פועלי ציון	laborer					x	808 פּוֹעֵל
	fruitful		x				809 פּוֹרָה

"Cognates"	English Equivalent	Category					Word
		C	F	B₃	B₂	B₁	
א פחד	fear				x		810 פַּחַד
	less					x	811 פָּחוֹת
	hammer		x				812 פַּטִּישׁ
	his mouth	x					813 פִּיו
	he turned					x	814 פָּנָה
ראש פנה	corner				x		815 פִּנָּה
פנים	face					x	816 פָּנִים
פסח	Passover					x	817 פָּסַח
	action, activity				x		818 פְּעוּלָה
„הפועל", פועל'ן	he acted	x					819 פָּעַל
	once					x	820 פַּעַם
	a wound				x		821 פֶּצַע
	order	x					822 פְּקוּדָה
	official, clerk				x		823 פָּקִיד
	orange grove				x		824 פַּרְדֵּס
	cow					x	825 פָּרָה
פרוטה	small coin				x		826 פְּרוּטָה
	flower					x	827 פֶּרַח
א פרט	individual					x	828 פְּרָט
	private				x		829 פְּרָטִי
פירות	fruit				x		830 פְּרִי
פרנסה	livelihood				x		831 פַּרְנָסָה
פשוט	simple				x		832 פָּשׁוּט
	suddenly					x	833 פִּתְאוֹם
	he opened					x	834 פָּתַח

"Cognates"	English Equivalent	Category					Word
		C	F	B₃	B₂	B₁	
פתח־תקוה	an opening	x					פֶּתַח 835
	note				x		פִּתְקָה 836
	small cattle	x					צֹאן 837
צבאי (ארגון צבאי לאומי)	army				x		צָבָא 838
	public				x		צִבּוּר 839
	color				x		צֶבַע 840
	justice					x	צָדָק 841
צדיק	righteous person				x		צַדִּיק 842
	yellow		x				צָהֹב 843
	noon					x	צָהֳרַיִם 844
	scout	x					צוֹפֶה 845
צורה	form				x		צוּרָה 846
	laughter				x		צְחוֹק 847
	he laughed				x		צָחַק 848
ציון	Zionist					x	צִיּוֹנִי 849
	plant				x		צֶמַח 850
	wool		x				צֶמֶר 851
	step					x	צַעַד 852
השומר הצעיר	young					x	צָעִיר 853
	he shouted					x	צָעַק 854
צער	sorrow				x		צַעַר 855
	north				x		צָפוֹן 856
	bird				x		צִפּוֹר 857
	narrow				x		צַר 858

"Cognates"	English Equivalent	C	F	B3	B2	B1	Word
צרה	trouble				x		צָרָה 859
א נצרך	it is necessary					x	צָרִיךְ 860
	necessity					x	צֹרֶךְ 861
	fixed					x	קָבוּעַ 862
קבוץ	a collective settlement				x		קְבוּץ 863
קבוצה	a group					x	קְבוּצָה 864
מקבל פנים	he received					x	קִבֵּל 865
קבלת פנים	receipt					x	קַבָּלָה 866
	he fixed					x	קָבַע 867
קודם כל	formerly	x					קֹדֶם 868
רוח הקודש	holiness					x	קֹדֶשׁ 869
ראש הקהל, קהלה	crowd	x					קָהָל 870
	he hoped					x	קִוָּה 871
	voice					x	קוֹל 872
	small					x	קָטָן 873
קרן קיימת	he fulfilled	x					קִיֵּם 874
	summer		x				קַיִץ 875
	wall		x				קִיר 876
	light					x	קַל 877
	he got up					x	קָם 878
	flour					x	קֶמַח 879
	he bought					x	קָנָה 880
	cash					x	קֻפָּה 881
	jump		x				קְפִיצָה 882
	sick-fund	x					קֻפַּת־חוֹלִים 883

"Cognates"	English Equivalent	Category					Word
		C	F	B₃	B₂	B₁	
	edge					x	קָצֶה 884
	short					x	קָצָר 885
	a bit	x					קְצָת 886
	cold		x				קַר 887
	he read					x	קָרָא 888
	it happened					x	קָרָה 889
א קרוב	near					x	קָרוֹב 890
קרן קיימת	fund	x					קֶרֶן 891
(ניש) קשה	hard					x	קָשֶׁה 892
	connection					x	קָשֶׁר 893
	he saw					x	רָאָה 894
ראש השנה	head					x	רֹאשׁ 895
ראשון לציון	first					x	רִאשׁוֹן 896
	a beginning	x					רֵאשִׁית 897
	numerous	x					רַב 898
	majority					x	רֹב 899
רב	Rabbi	x					רַב 900
רבּי	Rabbi	x					רַבִּי 901
	a quarter				x		רֶבַע 902
	foot					x	רֶגֶל 903
רגע	moment					x	רֶגַע 904
	a feeling				x		רָגָשׁ 905
	rifle				x		רוֹבֶה 906
רוח הקודש	spirit					x	רוּחַ 907
	wind				x		רוּחַ 908
	shepherd					x	רוֹעֶה 909

"Cognates"	English Equivalent	Category					Word
		C	F	B₃	B₂	B₁	
א רפואה	physician					x	רוֹפֵא 910
	broad				x		רָחָב 911
	street					x	רְחוֹב 912
	far					x	רָחוֹק 913
מרחץ	he washed				x		רָחַץ 914
	smell				x		רֵיחַ 915
	empty				x		רֵיק 916
	soft				x		רַךְ 917
	he rode					x	רָכַב 918
	train					x	רַכֶּבֶת 919
	property				x		רְכוּשׁ 920
	bad					x	רַע 921
	companion		x				רֵעַ 922
	he tended (sheep·)		x				רָעָה (צֹאן) 923
רעשׁ	noise				x		רַעַשׁ 924
	he wanted					x	רָצָה 925
	will (n.)					x	רָצוֹן 926
	attached		x				רָצוּף 927
	only					x	רַק 928
	he danced				x		רָקַד 929
	permission					x	רְשׁוּת 930
	list					x	רְשִׁימָה 931
	impression				x		רֹשֶׁם 932
	he asked					x	שָׁאַל 933
א שאלה	question					x	שָׁאֵלָה 934

"Cognates"	English Equivalent	C	F	B₃	B₂	B₁	Word
חג השבועות	week					x	935 שָׁבוּעַ
שבעה עשר בתמוז	seven (m.)					x	936 שִׁבְעָה
	satisfied					x	937 שְׂבַעְרָצוֹן
	he broke			x			938 שָׁבַר
שבת	Sabbath					x	939 שַׁבָּת
	mistake		x				940 שְׁגִיאָה
	field					x	941 שָׂדֶה
	again		x				942 שׁוּב
	policeman					x	943 שׁוֹטֵר
(קיין) שום (זאך)	nothing		x				944 שׁוּם (שׁוּם דָּבָר)
שונא	enemy	x					945 שׂוֹנֵא
	different					x	946 שׁוֹנֶה
א שופט	judge					x	947 שׁוֹפֵט
	black			x			948 שָׁחוֹר
שטר	bill		x				949 שְׁטָר
	conversation					x	950 שִׂיחָה
	belonging to			x			951 שֶׁיָּךְ
	singing					x	952 שִׁירָה
	he lay down					x	953 שָׁכַב
	quarter, neighborhood					x	954 שְׁכוּנָה
שכור	drunk	x					955 שִׁכּוֹר
	he forgot					x	956 שָׁכַח
שכן, שכנות	neighbor					x	957 שָׁכֵן
שכר	wages					x	958 שָׂכָר
	of					x	959 שֶׁל

"Cognates"	English Equivalent	Category					Word
		C	F	B3	B2	B1	
	snow				x		שֶׁלֶג 960
שלום עליכם	hello! (*lit.*, peace)					x	שָׁלוֹם 961
	he sent					x	שָׁלַח 962
„שולחן ערוך"	table				x		שֻׁלְחָן 963
יעמוד שלישי	third (m.)					x	שְׁלִישִׁי 964
	he paid					x	שָׁלֵם 965
	complete					x	שָׁלֵם 966
שלש סעודות	three (m.)					x	שְׁלֹשָׁה 967
	thirty					x	שְׁלֹשִׁים 968
	there					x	שָׁם 969
בעל שם טוב, א שם	name					x	שֵׁם 970
	left		x				שְׂמֹאל 971
	eight (m.)					x	שְׁמוֹנָה 972
	he was glad					x	שָׂמַח 973
שמחת תורה, בעל שמחה	joy					x	שִׂמְחָה 974
	sky					x	שָׁמַיִם 975
	dress		x				שִׂמְלָה 976
	oil					x	שֶׁמֶן 977
	cream					x	שַׁמֶּנֶת 978
„שמע ישראל"	he heard					x	שָׁמַע 979
השומר הצעיר	he kept					x	שָׁמַר 980
	sun					x	שֶׁמֶשׁ 981
שנה טובה	year					x	שָׁנָה 982
	sleep		x				שֵׁנָה 983

"Cognates"	English Equivalent	Category					Word
		C	F	B₃	B₂	B₁	
	second (m.)					x	שֵׁנִי 984
	two					x	שְׁנַיִם 985
	teeth					x	שִׁנַּיִם 986
שעה	hour					x	שָׁעָה 987
	watch, clock		x				שָׁעוֹן 988
	lesson					x	שִׁעוּר 989
	gate					x	שַׁעַר 990
	language	x					שָׂפָה 991
	sack					x	שַׂק 992
	quietness			x			שֶׁקֶט 993
שקר	lie (n.)			x			שֶׁקֶר 994
	he sang			x			שָׁר 995
	six (m.)					x	שִׁשָּׁה 996
	sixth					x	שִׁשִּׁי 997
	he drank					x	שָׁתָה 998
	two (f.)					x	שְׁתַּיִם 999
	he described	x					תֵּאֵר 1000
	box					x	תֵּבָה 1001
	demand	x					תְּבִיעָה 1002
	P.O.B. (post office box)	x					ת. ד. (תֵּבַת־ דֹּאַר) 1003
	thanks					x	תּוֹדָה 1004
	outcome					x	תּוֹצָאָה 1005
	produce					x	תּוֹצֶרֶת 1006
	queue, line			x			תּוֹר 1007
תורה	study					x	תּוֹרָה 1008

"Cognates"	English Equivalent	Category					Word
		C	F	B₃	B₂	B₁	
	station					x	תַּחֲנָה 1009
תחת (חלק הגוף האחורי)	under					x	תַּחַת 1010
	contents				x		תֹּכֶן 1011
	program					x	תָּכְנִית 1012
תיכף	immediately					x	תֵּכֶף 1013
תלמיד חכם	pupil					x	תַּלְמִיד 1014
	picture					x	תְּמוּנָה 1015
	always					x	תָּמִיד 1016
	give!					x	תֵּן 1017
תנאים לחתונה	condition					x	תְּנַאי 1018
	movement					x	תְּנוּעָה 1019
	certificate					x	תְּעוּדָה 1020
	apple				x		תַּפּוּחַ 1021
	potato				x		תַּפּוּחַ־אֲדָמָה 1022
	orange			x			תַּפּוּחַ־זָהָב 1023
שיר „התקוה"	hope					x	תִּקְוָה 1024
	he repaired					x	תִּקֵּן 1025
בעל תשובה	answer					x	תְּשׁוּבָה 1026
	attention					x	תְּשׂוּמֶת־לֵב 1027
	payment					x	תַּשְׁלוּם 1028
תשעה באב	nine (m.)					x	תִּשְׁעָה 1029

NOTES TO CHAPTER FOUR

1. Some sixty per cent of all research work in the field of language teaching during the years 1930-1937 was devoted to the problem of vocabulary. See *Encyclopedia of Educational Research* (1950), p. 528.

2. Handschin, *op. cit.*, p. 173.

3. Kaeding, J. W., *Häufigkeitswörterbuch der deutschen Sprache* (1898).

4. Thorndike, E. L., *The Teacher's Word Book* (1921 and later editions).

5. Horne, Ernest, *A Basic Writing Vocabulary*: 10,000 *Words Most Commonly Used in Writing* (1926).

6. Rieger, E., *Basic Word List of Everyday Hebrew* (1935) (in Hebrew).

7. Brill, M., in collaboration with D. Neustadt and P. Schusser, *The Basic Word List of the Arabic Daily Newspaper* (1940) (in Hebrew).

8. The above table lists the frequency of only 2,000 Hebrew words whereas Thorndike's book lists the frequency of 20,000 words and in its 1944 revision by Thorndike and Lorge it lists 30,000 words. The number of words in the Hebrew frequency list was limited for statistical reasons. Thorndike's count was based on five million running words, and in the 1944 revision on nine million; but the Hebrew count was based on only 200,000 running words. Words occurring less than 10 times were not included in the Hebrew frequency list.

9. The ten most common words in Hebrew are: אמר, היה, זה, של, על, כל, לא, את, כי, אותו. They make up only 12 per cent of the vocabulary as compared with English where the first ten words make up 25 per cent. The explanation is that Hebrew uses prefixes for "the," "and," "in," "like," "as," "to," "for," "from," "that," "which," "who," etc., and our list contains only full words.

10. Washburne, C. W., "A Spelling Curriculum Based on Research," *Elementary School Journal*, v. 23 (1923) pp. 752ff.

11. Handschin, *op. cit.*, p. 166.

12. Though 50 is not a large number, it is "a desirable minimum for experimental work" if the sampling is well chosen, see Holzinger, K. J., *Statistical Methods for Students in Education* (1928), p. 3f.

13. Our Basic Word List, which contains the 2,017 most frequent words of everyday Hebrew, was discussed in a number of reviews and articles. Several textbook writers used the word list to aid them in selecting the vocabulary for their texts. There was some negative criticism centering on three points:

1) The fact that the count was based to such a large extent on letters written by school children and on private and business letters written by adults whose knowledge of Hebrew was none too perfect, instead of being based on classic and modern Hebrew literature and on the daily press.

2) The lack of certain words which the critics felt to be very frequent and which they found in the first or second thousand words in the Thorndike list.

3) The fact that the sampling was not sufficient from the statistical point of view.

Since I have not yet had occasion to answer these criticisms, I should like to take this opportunity to discuss them in some detail.

1) I do not regret the fact that I did not use literary sources and newspapers to a greater extent in my frequency count. On the contrary, I regret having used them at all. If I were undertaking a frequency count of everyday Hebrew again, I would base my work on letters and on the spoken language, and I would not use, as I did earlier, selections from the Bible, Agada, the Prayer-book, etc. Literary sources are being used less and less in frequency counts. It is not a question of making the work easier. It is easier to make word counts in classical Hebrew literature where very full concordances are available. We must remember that our primary concern is to determine what words are current in colloquial Hebrew as used in Israel today, and not what words were most frequent in the Bible, Agada, or are most frequent in modern Hebrew literature.

2) The fact that a critic may find certain words omitted which seem to him essential scarcely invalidates the count. Such an objection merely shows that the critic in question has little faith in word counts as an objective means of determining the most frequent words. One critic selected a portion from a children's Hebrew newspaper, one from the Agada and one from the Bible, and attempted to prove that the first 2,000 words in the *Basic Word List* included only 70 per cent of the words found in the portion chosen from a children's newspaper and the one chosen from the Agada, and only 60 per cent of the words in the portion chosen from the Bible. This is not a serious criticism since the three selections contain only 236 words and all the three passages are of a literary nature. If the critic found two-thirds of the words within the first 2,000 words of our Word List, we have an indication that the first 2,000 words in the list provide an excellent basis for the study of both the older literary sources and of modern literature. The fact that the critic found several words in the first 2,000 entries of the Hebrew Word List which are not in Thorndike's list is not at all surprising. This is a common phenomenon. We find the very same thing if we compare, for example, the two large frequency dictionaries of Thorndike and Horne, both for English.

3) It would undoubtedly have been better to double or triple the number of running words, but 200,000 running words provide

a valuable sampling if they are taken from the right sources (see French, W. C., "A Study of Children's Letters," *The Nation at Work on the Public School Curriculum,* Fourth Yearbook, Department of Superintendence, 1926, pp. 144-145). The nature of the material used is more important than the number of words counted. "We may well wonder why millions of words are being tabulated while more important factors are being neglected." In any event, we may be reasonably certain, as I pointed out above, that the first 738 words of our list (each with a frequency of 50 or over) are the most frequent words in the language. We cannot be as certain about the remaining words, for the reliability of the list decreases as the frequency of the words decreases. Much as I should like to see a study made using a larger sampling, I doubt its feasibility at the moment, and I question its desirability in view of the fact that *frequency* studies are giving way at present to studies of the *basic* words in a language.

14. Cole, R. D. and Tharp, J. B., *Modern Foreign Languages and Their Teaching* (1937), p. 568f.

15. Ogden, C. K., *The Basic Dictionary* (1939) and *Basic Step by Step* (1935). "Basic" in this connection stands for British, American, Scientific, International, Commercial.

16. When there are two or more synonyms, the basic list selects the most frequent word but not invariably so. Thus the word כאן selected for "here" rather than פה, because it covers the concept of both "place" and "motion towards" whereas פה does not cover the latter meaning.

17. Basic English does not include, for example, the common words "can" or "must" since the idea "can" may be expressed by "be able," and "must" by "have to" or "is necessary."

18. Since Basic English includes only 18 verbs, other verbs have to be expressed by one of the basic verbs plus a noun; instead of "to fall" Basic English uses "to have a fall," etc.

19. e. g., instead of "tent," Basic English uses "canvas house." We could also do the same in Hebrew, except that the word "tent" is so much more important in Hebrew that it is included in the list of basic words.

20. *Encyclopedia of Educational Research* (1941), p. 529f.

21. Handschin, *op. cit.,* 161ff.

22. We cannot speak of "cognate" between English and French, say, and Hebrew. But we can, on the other hand, make use of a few Hebrew words that have been borrowed by the European languages or words which are mnemotechnically or etymologically connected (i.e., where both the European languages and Hebrew have borrowed the same word from Greek, Arabic, Persian, etc.). In the Basic Hebrew Word List we find the following examples: אויר, אוירון and *air;* ארגון and *organization;* יהודי and *Judean;* יין and *wine;* כרטיס and *card;* מברשת and *brush;* מכונה, מכונית and *machine;* סבון and *savon* (French), *soap;* סכר and *sugar;* עברי and *Hebrew;* ערבי and *Arab;* פרדס and *Paradise;* שבעה and *seven;* ששה and *six;* שׂק and *sack.*

23. It seemed clear to the writer that people who are ac-

quainted with "cognate" words in Yiddish and to whom the
Jewish, and/or the Israeli milieu is known, can study Hebrew
with greater ease. What was less clear to him was whether the
Jews in the Diaspora, after the destruction of East European
Jewry, are still acquainted with Yiddish expressions and with the
Jewish, and/or the Israeli milieu so that we can rely on such
knowledge in our teaching of Hebrew. There was room for
serious doubt as to whether the young generation, which studies or
is expected to study Hebrew, has acquired a satisfactory number of
such expressions.

In order to determine the situation, the writer asked for and
secured the co-operation of the Jewish Education Committee of
New York City, headed by Dr. Alexander M. Dushkin and, after
his departure to Israel, by Dr. Azriel Eizenberg. The author
composed a multiple-choice test of 128 Hebrew words on the
basis of a list of Hebrew words used in Yiddish, prepared by the
supervisor of the Jewish Education Committee, Mr. Yudel Mark,
and other available material. The multiple choice test contained
62 words used in Yiddish and another 66 expressions common
in the Jewish, and/or the Israeli milieu. This test was administered by Mrs. Augusta Saretsky, Consultant on Parent Education,
and Mr. Bortniker, Supervisor of the Jewish Education Committee, to 336 examinees, out of whom 216 were boys and girls of
school age (up to 18 years old) and 113 adults (over 31 years
old). Except for four people aged 19 to 30, who happened
to take part in the test, the examinees were of two age groups,
namely, youngsters and adults, with a chronological range of half
a generation or a generation between them. This arrangement
was made especially in order to test the different degrees of
knowledge of "cognate" words by the young generation of today
as compared with their elders. The scoring of the material of the
test was done by the statistical unit of the Jewish Education
Committee under the direction of Mr. J. M. Horden. I give here
the results, as summarized by Mr. Horden, under three heads: a)
personal data on the examinees; b) results achieved in the knowledge of Hebrew words, compared with the knowledge of Yiddish;
c) the knowledge of 128 Hebrew words by youngsters and adults.

Personal Data on the Examinees

Number of examinees: 336, personal data answered by 333.
*Age*s Under 18 years old, 216; 31 years and over, 113; 19-30
year old, 4.
Sex: Male, 99; female, 234.
Country of Birth: U.S.A., 294; other countries, 39.
General Education: Elementary School in the U. S., 311; abroad,
22. Secondary Education in the U.S., 319; abroad, 10.
Jewish Education: All Day School, 23; Afternoon School, 185;
Sunday School, 66.

The majority of the examinees, then, were born in the United
States and were educated in American schools; 7 per cent at-
tended Jewish all day schools; 55 per cent, Jewish afternoon

schools; 20 per cent, Jewish Sunday schools; and 18 per cent received no Jewish education whatsoever. From what we know about Jewish education in the United States, and in New York in particular, these examinees were on a higher level as far as their Jewish and general education is concerned, than the average Jew in the United States. The congregational affiliation of the examinees—they belonged to 9 Orthodox, 5 Conservative and 3 Reform Synagogues—is perhaps another indication that we have here youngsters and adults who in terms of adherence to Judaism are more active than the average. The examiners belong therefore to those circles from which come most of the students of Hebrew.

A comparison between the data showing the knowledge of the examinees in Yiddish and their understanding of Hebrew words is illustrated by the following table:

Achievement in Understanding 128 Hebrew Words as Compared to the Knowledge of Yiddish

a) The Understanding of 62 Hebrew Words Used in Yiddish

No. of questions answered correctly	Under 18 years old			31 years and older		
	Knows Yiddish well	Knows Yiddish fairly well	Doesn't know Yiddish	Knows Yiddish well	Knows Yiddish fairly well	Doesn't know Yiddish
0-10	—	14	15	1	—	4
11-20	2	25	5	—	3	4
21-30	5	29	4	—	7	2
31-40	10	13	2	2	15	4
41-50	19	14	10	11	13	2
51-60	26	17	5	24	8	3
61-63	—	1	—	9	1	—
Total	62	113	41	47	47	19
Average of correct answers	45	29	25	56	39	28

b) The Understanding of 66 Hebrew Words Common in Jewish and Israeli Milieu

0-10	1	8	1	1	3	1
11-20	2	17	7	—	2	—
21-30	9	23	8	1	3	7
31-40	14	32	11	4	6	4
41-50	13	15	8	13	14	4
51-60	17	14	4	15	14	2
61-63	6	4	2	13	5	1
Total	62	113	41	47	47	19
Average of Correct answers	43	34	34	51	43	36

The results indicate the following: a) The understanding of 128 Hebrew words used in Yiddish and in connection with Jewish and Israeli life is on the whole quite significant, and it is worthwhile to utilize this knowledge in the teaching of Hebrew. b) The achievements of the examinees who do not know Yiddish are at least half as good as the achievements of those who know Yiddish well, while the difference between the two groups in their knowledge of Hebrew expressions taken from Jewish or Israeli life is even smaller, the proportion between them being 1:2/3. c) The achievements of the adults are on the whole higher than those of the youngsters to an extent of 15 to 20 per cent.

Details about the knowledge of 128 Hebrew words are furnished in the following table:

Knowledge of 128 Hebrew Words by Youngsters and Adults
Part 1: 62 Hebrew Words Used in Yiddish

No.	Word	No. of Examinees under 18 years who answered			No. of Examinees over 31 years who answered		
		Right	Wrong	No Answer	Right	Wrong	No Answer
1	אוודאי	147	7	65	96	7	12
2	אמת	171	10	38	104	1	10
3	אפילו	130	34	55	78	22	15
4	אפשר	182	2	35	105	—	10
5	בחור	138	23	58	95	7	13
6	בעל בית	139	50	30	99	12	4
7	בעל מלאכה	81	42	96	71	8	36
8	בקשה	107	18	94	55	8	52
9	בשעת	57	40	122	43	20	52
10	גנב	172	4	43	109	—	6
11	דיינו	77	71	71	81	6	28
12	דוקא	29	73	117	23	53	39
13	דירה	54	36	129	48	11	56
14	חבר	160	10	49	96	1	18
15	חברה	87	40	92	98	4	13
16	חדר	179	17	23	108	1	6
17	חדש	153	23	43	80	12	23
18	חוצפה	118	32	69	110	2	3
19	חיה	137	18	64	90	4	21
20	חכם	164	22	33	99	4	12
21	חלום	162	6	51	90	2	23
22	חלק	119	15	85	80	—	35
23	חן	99	33	87	96	2	17
24	חשבון	47	61	111	66	19	30
25	חשוב	82	20	117	45	11	59
26	טובה	140	16	63	96	1	18
27	טעות	63	24	132	53	5	57
28	כבוד	141	13	65	103	1	11

No.	Word	No. of Examinees under 18 years who answered			No. of Examinees over 31 years who answered		
		Right	Wrong	No Answer	Wrong	Right	No Answer
29	כדי	108	22	89	58	12	45
30	כח	159	10	50	95	2	18
31	כוס	93	44	82	62	22	31
32	כיבוד	53	19	147	50	6	59
33	כל זמן	121	17	81	66	2	47
34	כמעט	92	23	104	69	5	41
35	לכבוד	143	6	70	97	2	16
36	מזרח	126	29	64	60	10	45
37	מין	74	37	108	48	11	56
38	מלחמה	154	8	57	92	5	18
39	מציאה	82	40	97	106	1	8
40	משוגע	190	2	27	107	—	8
41	משל	91	30	98	70	7	38
42	משפחה	159	13	47	105	—	10
43	מתנה	133	12	74	82	4	29
44	נביא	118	24	77	77	6	32
45	גיש קשה	45	47	127	38	29	48
46	סביבה	66	41	112	29	10	76
47	סוחר	72	28	119	55	5	55
48	סוף	149	13	57	89	5	21
49	סחורה	103	10	106	78	2	35
50	סכנה	65	25	129	41	11	63
51	עוף	72	33	114	42	8	65
52	עין הרע	73	43	103	74	12	29
53	פנים	171	10	38	106	7	8
54	צרה	126	11	82	102	—	13
55	קודם כל	106	23	90	65	15	35
56	קרוב	81	22	116	50	6	59
57	רגע	111	16	92	47	5	63
58	שאלה	134	16	69	90	7	18
59	שונא	115	15	89	96	2	17
60	שכור	175	6	38	108	1	6
61	שמחה	166	18	35	102	3	10
62	שעה	107	21	91	76	9	30

Part 2: 66 *Expressions Used in Jewish and Israeli Milieu*

No.	Word	No. of Examinees under 18 years who answered			No. of Examinees over 31 years who answered		
		Right	Wrong	No Answer	Right	Wrong	No Answer
1	אגודת ישראל	65	68	86	49	30	36
2	אחד העם	31	76	112	47	15	53
3	ארבע כוסות	147	13	59	75	7	33
4	ארגון צבאי לאומי	130	21	68	79	9	27
5	ארץ ישראל	212	2	5	104	2	9
6	ברכה	180	4	35	103	—	12
7	גלות	96	40	83	72	11	32
8	גן עדן	171	5	43	93	2	20
9	דרך ארץ	81	27	111	54	6	55
10	הבימה	121	41	57	77	9	29
11	הגדה	179	16	24	100	6	9
12	הגנה	196	7	16	106	—	9
13	הסתדרות	91	28	100	80	9	26
14	השומר הצעיר	44	66	109	37	17	61
15	התקוה	200	2	17	105	—	10
16	חלוץ	180	11	28	83	5	27
17	חמשה עשר	90	50	79	87	3	25
18	חסיד	57	56	106	40	41	34
19	חתן	155	15	49	103	1	11
20	יום כפור	207	--	12	107	—	8
21	ימים נוראים	47	47	125	42	16	57
22	ישוב	87	34	98	65	22	28
23	ישיבה	184	6	29	105	—	10
24	כלה	135	11	73	101	2	12
25	כשר	201	2	16	105	—	10
26	לחיים	154	17	48	96	7	12
27	לשון הרע	85	20	114	38	15	62
28	מזל טוב	195	5	19	105	—	10
29	מזרחי	135	12	72	97	2	16
30	מלמד	92	26	101	96	2	17
31	נגב	152	31	36	89	8	18
32	סדר	195	3	21	107	—	8
33	ספר	201	1	17	97	2	16
34	עונג שבת	77	81	61	73	24	18
35	עליה	78	34	107	49	27	39
36	עלית נוער	60	15	144	40	8	67
37	עם הארץ	53	59	107	40	25	50
38	עמק	129	23	67	50	3	62
39	ערב יום טוב	161	17	41	96	2	17
40	ערב שבת	173	9	37	97	3	15
41	פועלי ציון	62	20	137	71	3	41
42	פרנסה	66	43	110	86	9	20
43	פתח תקוה	76	37	106	57	10	48
44	קבוץ	113	17	89	80	5	30
45	קבוצה	86	17	116	59	9	47

No.	Word	No. of Examinees under 18 years who answered			No. of Examinees over 31 years who answered		
		Right	Wrong	No Answer	Wrong	Right	No Answer
46	קרן היסוד	82	13	124	76	5	34
47	קרן קיימת	100	6	113	68	1	46
48	ראש השנה	176	3	40	101	—	14
49	ראש חודש	157	5	57	93	—	22
50	ראש פנה	21	56	142	28	22	65
51	ראשון לציון	45	40	134	42	14	59
52	רב	115	10	94	91	9	15
53	שבועות	128	22	69	87	8	20
54	שבת	171	5	43	97	—	18
55	שלום	177	6	36	98	2	15
56	שלום עליכם	131	45	43	76	26	13
57	שלחן ערוך	78	19	122	52	12	51
58	שמונה עשרה	116	14	89	78	2	35
59	שמע	129	6	84	89	4	22
60	שמחת תורה	154	11	54	98	2	15
61	תורה	151	30	38	94	10	11
62	תל־אביב	177	4	38	85	2	28
63	תלמוד תורה	141	31	47	95	7	13
64	תלמיד חכם	135	10	74	77	6	32
65	תפילין	131	16	72	96	4	15
66	תשעה באב	110	36	73	93	7	15

The above table indicates clearly that familiarity with Yiddish has no decisive effect on the knowledge of Hebrew expressions adopted from Jewish religious tradition and Israeli life. It would appear therefore that in spite of the decline of Yiddish among the Jewish masses, Jewish tradition and the new life in Israel have retained their position as influential factors in the dissemination of Hebrew expressions.

24. Shortly before publication of this book I received from Mr. Nahshon who is preparing his doctoral dissertation at Teachers' College, Columbia University, on the Vocabulary of Essential Hebrew—very helpful comments based on a painstaking comparison between my Frequency Word List and my Vocabularly of Essential Hebrew. As a result of his comments, I decided to add to the 198 word of high frequency, not included in the Basic Word List, eleven more words, as follows:

אליהם (to them), אליו (to him), אשתו (his wife), התפלל (he prayed), חשמל (electricity), יחס (relationship), יעשה (he has been), נעשה (respectable), נכבד (angel), מלאך (will make), צד (side), (made

The number of words in Category F will thus be increased to 209, and the total of words included in my Vocabulary of Essential Hebrew—to 1040 words.

My thanks to Mr. Sh. Nahshon for his comments.

CHAPTER FIVE

OLD AND NEW METHODS IN LANGUAGE TEACHING

The Translation Method

Language instruction for many centuries centered on three things: vocabulary, grammar and translation work. Vocabulary furnished the raw material, grammar the tools for working this raw material up, and translation provided an opportunity for putting into active use the lexical and grammatical information acquired.

Educators considered translation to be excellent practice, for here was a meeting point of two languages and two cultures. It also had in their opinion an important disciplinary value: translation helped "train the mind" by requiring concentrated mental effort, exactness, consideration of fine shades of meaning in both languages involved, etc. Goethe, whose approach to language teaching was remarkably modern in many regards, remarks [1] that there are two principles in translation: "One requires that the foreign author should be presented to us in such a form that we can consider him one of our own; the second requires that we try to enter into the spirit of the foreign author and understand his qualities of mind and appreciate his use of language." Goethe came to the conclusion that we must steer a middle course and try to satisfy both principles by making adjustments from both ends. This can only be done if we translate not words but content. The difficulty inherent in all translation work is well expressed in the cynical aphorism which compared a translation to a woman: "If beautiful she is not faithful, if faithful she is not beautiful." [2]

Many conservative teachers still maintain that the best way to teach a language is through exact verbal translation. Indeed this argument is still used by those who wish to continue the study of Latin in the schools. They hold that our students can best learn to use their mother tongue correctly and effectively through translation work from a foreign language, particularly one which differs so greatly from their own as Latin does. But

127

the modern conception of the place of translation in language
teaching is different. We no longer believe that word-for-word
translations enable the student to derive the maximum enjoy-
ment from a text.[3] A good translator does not try to find words
in his mother tongue which match the words in the text before
him. He tries rather to get at the ideas expressed and to
render them in his own language.[4] Needless to say, the better
command he has of both languages, the easier it will be for him
to find the proper equivalents in each case. According to
Jespersen,[5] translation is for the teacher the easiest and for the
student the most certain and rapid way of enabling him to
understand a foreign language. Translation is the easiest way
for the student to show that he has understood a passage.
Practice in translation also makes the student aware of semantic
problems and helps him avoid ambiguity and inexactness.
Many educators have held that the translation method is more
effective than any other in developing in the student the ability
to read and write the language.[6] Translation served as the
underlining method of the well known "Toussaint-Langenscheidt Letters for Self-Teaching" which were much in vogue
at the end of the 19th and the beginning of the 20th centuries.
With German painstaking elaboration this Langenscheidt
method presented in 36 Letters to the Student an enormous
wealth of vocabulary (over 14,000 English words) and of grammar. In the very first Letters the student began to read literary
masterpieces. The Langenscheidt method was designed for
studious learners with a great deal of time at their disposal.
It was jokingly said of these Letters that whoever managed to
reach the last one was sure to acquire a good command of the
new language, unless before then he went out of his mind from
drudgery and despair. The analytical procedure of Langenscheidt—leading from the presentation of meaningful materials
conceived on broad lines, to the singling out of the component
parts for special treatment—was basically sound from the view-
point of modern psychology. But Langenscheidt's excessive
accumulation of lexically and grammatically difficult material,
his two-way translations (into and from the native tongue) and
his laborious drills overburdened with grammar, had on the
average student a bewildering and discouraging effect.

A counterpart to Langenscheidt for the self-teaching of
Hebrew were the 32 Letters composed by the gifted Hebrew
pedagogue, Shevach Walkowski, in Cracow, Poland (Walkowski

was murdered by the Nazis during the Second World War). He could claim to his credit that he probably taught modern Hebrew to more people than any other Hebrew teacher of his day.

The Army method, which will be described later on, used free translation to a certain extent. However Angiolillo in his *Armed Forces Foreign Language Teaching*[7] maintains on the basis of Army experience and other evidence, that the direct method is more effective than the translation method.

The principal objection to the translation method is that it sets up an artificial barrier between the student and the language studied, whereas the direct method enables the student to think in the foreign language. Another objection is that many passages are extremely difficult to translate from one language to another.

Modified Form of the Translation Method

In order to meet these objections the translation method has been modified in the light of recent advances in the pedagogy and psychology of language teaching. We may consider each of these improvements in some detail.

1) The gradual elimination of translation is one of the most important principles in this modified form of the translation method. After the students have used this method for a time, translation is gradually eliminated, first for short, easy sentences and then for longer passages. After a while the students begin to read texts without consulting the translation, or consulting it as little as possible. Even where they encounter individual words which they do not know, it is better for them to try to guess the meaning from the context and only after they have finished the whole passage to consult the translation to see if their guess was correct. In this way the student relies less and less on translation and begins to think in the foreign language. Translations must be used in some measure, as we shall later have occasion to point out. Even in the direct method it is not eliminated entirely. The translation may be indirect and subvocal but it is still there.

2) We have already mentioned that where translation is used, semantic units should be translated and not isolated words. The objection that many things cannot be translated from one language to another is a valid one, particularly if one tries to translate each word; for many words and expressions in one

language may not have exact parallels in another. However, the work of the translator is much easier if he tries to render the semantic content of sentences or whole passages.[8] Concentrating on these larger units rather than on individual words is also to be recommended from the standpoint of proper reading habits, since the eye span covers not individual words but entire units.

3) Translation should be always in one direction, that is, from the foreign language to one's own language. It is psychologically unsound [9] to try to translate into a foreign language before one has an adequate command of it. Experiments have shown that when material is translated into one's own language the recall is two or three times greater than when material is translated into a foreign language.[10] Translating into a foreign language may be justified in an intensive course where it is possible to ask students to undertake all sorts of difficult assignments, but in other cases if translation into a foreign language is given, it should be confined to stereotyped business letters and the like.[11]

4) Translation drills excessively loaded with grammatical material should definitely be discarded. Translation of this sort does not give the student active command of the grammatical material or even a passive recognition of the grammatical features.[12]

5) The teacher must systematically point out the differences and resemblances between the two languages. It is true that some linguistically gifted students may here and there notice by themselves similarities and differences of idioms and grammatical constructions. But even such students need to have their attention directed to each important point as it is met. Transfer of training from the mother tongue to a foreign language is not automatic; but when consciously directed by the teacher, it can be exercised even on a play level as an enjoyable and beneficial linguistic sport. This is particularly true in the case of closely related languages such as Hebrew and Arabic where there are many expressions which are similar but not identical in the two languages.

Anyone teaching Hebrew as a living language should be acquainted with the language of his pupils and should seize every opportunity to point out the differences and the similarities between the two languages.

In pedagogical literature the formal grammar method and

the translation method are always discussed together, as though they were one system, or at least complementary systems. Actually there is no connection. Whereas the teaching of formal grammar has been unsuccessful in modern language instruction, the translation method has met with a considerable degree of success. Both methods may have in common the fact that they have long been in use, but that is the only connection between them. Even in the teaching of Latin there has been an important change, and in recent years attempts have been made to stress the translation method and to pay little attention to composition.[13] The translation method is especially suitable for use with mature students.[14] It has been found that such students retain the material better when the translation method is used than when audio-visual aids are stressed. Audio-visual aids on the other hand work best with children.

The Natural and Direct Methods of Language Teaching

There are scores of methods in use today which claim to be "natural" methods. All of them are united in their opposition to any type of translation and advocate the living approach to a language as the natural and best method of teaching. These methods differ very little in theory and even less in actual practice.[15] The "Reform Movement" in language instruction, which did away with the systematic presentation of grammar and which concentrated on spoken language and on the imitation of the teacher's speech, became known in Germany towards the end of the 19th Century. It was followed by other natural methods, the best known of which is that of Berlitz[16] which insisted that one should learn a foreign language the way a child learns his mother tongue—first learn to talk, then to read, and only later on approach the study of grammar. The teacher who uses one of these natural methods points to objects, calls them by their names, asks questions and answers them himself and then asks his pupils questions which they are to reply to, makes various movements and gestures, uses drawings and illustrations, pantomines and contrasts, and tries to get the student to imitate him as closely as possible. These devices are followed even at present by the Berlitz School (which incidentally today includes the study of Hebrew in its branches in Israel and elsewhere).

At the end of the 19th Century and the beginning of the 20th two methods originated in France and spread to other countries, namely, *la méthode Gouin* and *la méthode directe*. The Gouin method, commonly known also as the "series method," consists in following out a systematic sequence of topics, covering broad fields of general interest, such as home, school, community, occupations, farm and the like. The topics and sub-topics are treated much too fully for beginners and many uncommon words are included. Though the sentences tend to be useful, the vocabulary load is excessive (or, as we would say today, there are too many words which would not appear in frequency or basic lists). Gouin's methodological pattern has no consistent counterpart in Hebrew, but it was partly adapted by a number of Hebrew text book-writers who included, inter alia, some descriptions of everyday life with a vocabulary too specialized for the beginner.

The "direct" method has had an even greater vogue. It makes use of the techniques devised by the methods that preceded it and has placed more emphasis than either Berlitz or Gouin upon correct pronunciation and grammar. It stresses all four aspects of language learning—understanding of the spoken language, speaking, reading and writing [17]—and it eliminates the use of the mother tongue and all translation work. The method concentrates first on the spoken language, then on reading and finally on writing. Since the teacher is not supposed to use the student's native language, he often has to be something of an actor and a blackboard artist to get the meaning across.[18]

Limitations of the Direct Method

It is obvious that the use of the direct method limits the amount of grammatical material that can be presented, since even the grammatical rules have to be explained in the foreign language. The effectiveness of the direct method has been investigated in several studies. One of them [19] showed that 70 per cent of the students do not directly associate the foreign word with the object it represents, but use the process of silent translation. If it is true that the method does not lead to a direct association between the word and the object, then the "directness" of the method is debatable, and indeed the psychological foundations of the direct method are open to question. The psychological principle advanced by William James that in order to establish a new habit one has first to break the old habit, does not apply to the language learning situation, except where the student can go to the foreign country. It is very difficult to eliminate the native language when the student hears it about him all day. It requires a very talented teacher, and even then he cannot hope to succeed completely. By means of extensive exercises and drills he can teach his students scores and even hundreds of expressions and linguistic patterns which they can use without thinking of the translation. However the number of forms which the student can learn in this way is too limited. The teacher employing the direct method can teach concrete nouns, prepositions and verbs,[20] since he can point to objects, show pictures and relations, perform various actions, etc. He cannot of course be certain that the students always understand him correctly and know that he means "forehead" and not "head," or "water" and not "glass." There is always the danger that the students may get the wrong meaning, or not be certain of just what the teacher means. Teachers experienced in using the direct method can reduce to a minimum the number of these misunderstandings. Teachers new to the method often find it difficult to tell when the students have misinterpreted their meanings.

Here we touch upon an important point—the fact that we have both very gifted language teachers and teachers who are less so. This difference is important no matter what method is used, but it is particularly important when the method used is the direct one. A mediocre teacher can succeed with a translation method, but it is doubtful whether he could succeed with the direct method. Teachers need special training in order to employ the direct method successfully. One of the reasons why many schools did not adopt this method was that they did not have the proper personnel. In order to use the direct method the teacher must be able to speak the language fluently and, unfortunately, all too many language teachers do not meet this requirement.[21] Then, too, since the method requires the teacher to illustrate all sorts of actions and to make all sorts of gestures, it is more difficult to maintain classroom discipline.

Another disadvantage of the direct method is that it is hard to make homework assignments. This disadvantage looms largest with adult classes, since older students can learn as much from what they do outside of class as from their work in class.

Many of the teaching techniques used by the direct method remind one of the techniques used in kindergarten and the primary grades. As a matter of fact the direct method is most successful with children; although adolescent students and adults can also profit considerably from the techniques employed by the direct method.[22] The combination of sensory and motor impressions makes the method interesting to children and to a certain degree also to adults.

The method has been used successfully in Israeli schools. In general the teachers who meet with particular success are those trained in the kindergarten and primary grades.

The Aural-Oral Approach

There can be little doubt that the direct method helped to revitalize language instruction. Part of the success of the method may be ascribed to the enthusiasm of the teachers who used it. However, part of the success is doubtlessly due to the method itself.

Many consider the basic feature of the system to be the aural-oral approach and look upon its other features as of secondary importance.[23] The direct method concentrates at the outset on speech and dispenses not only with written work but even with reading practice. In the first stages it utilizes the ear and not the eye.[24] It considers the spoken language as primary and the written language as secondary.[25] When the Turks substituted the Latin for the Arabic alphabet in 1928 they continued to speak Turkish in exactly the same way: they merely began to use different symbols to represent the sounds. In order to be able to read silently or to write, one has to learn the alphabetic symbols of the language; but in order to learn to speak, one has only to listen carefully to the language and to imitate what one hears. On the other hand if one learns to read a language without learning the sounds one can never really understand the syntactical and morphological structure of the language. In teaching a foreign language, therefore, it is necessary to begin with practice in hearing and speaking. Regardless of whether our goal is a speaking or a reading knowledge of a language, we still have to begin with the spoken language. In order to gain command of the language we have to be able to speak; we can scarcely be said to have command of a language if we can only read it. "The speech is the language. The written record is but secondary." [26]

This point of view is basically sound, but too extreme in several respects. One cannot compare writing with musical notation,[27] and conclude that the written letters have no value in themselves, just as the musical notes have no value except when one sings or plays them on an instrument. This comparison certainly does not hold true of civilized societies, where the written language is of immense importance and has developed almost as an independent means of communication, parallel to the spoken language, the two forms of language—the spoken and the written—influencing one another in many ways. In civilized societies the written language has been so perfected that it now serves as a convenient and rapid means of expressing and recording our thoughts.[27] By means of the written language the reader can become acquainted with the best that has been said and thought in his own society or in other societies throughout the world, both in his own age and in earlier ages, and he can do so whenever and wherever he finds it convenient. Not only that, but he can also read the written words three or four times faster than he could follow them if spoken.

The aural-oral method should therefore not be used exclusively, as some of its advocates urge; but it should be used to some extent in all foreign language teaching and it should certainly be used in the opening stages. Where it is used exclusively, however, it is likely to defeat its own purpose, for it requires by its very nature long mechanical drills which prove tiring to most students. The students must listen and repeat [28] and then keep repeating till they know each expression or sentence by heart. Less intelligence is required than patience. The method trains the ear but we are still left with the problem of training the eye—an entirely different but equally important problem.

We must recognize the basic importance of the aural-oral approach and demand that Hebrew teachers, like all other modern language teachers, have fluent command of the language they are teaching. Hebrew teachers should spend a year, or at least half a year, in Israel to perfect their pronunciation and their knowledge of colloquial Hebrew. It would also be desirable to include in our examinations in teachers' training schools sections dealing with oral expression.

Some Principles of the Army Method

For generations foreign languages have been taught with very small success. Students studied foreign languages for years without acquiring any real command of it. Yet the Army program was able to train men to speak and understand languages in a very short period of time. What accounts for the success of the Army method?

One of the foundations of the Army method was the aural-oral approach. The aural-oral method was used with great success during the last war at the universities and colleges which participated in the U. S. Army Intensive Language Program. Similar programs were carried out in other countries, notably Britain. These programs were designed to teach languages in a short period, usually six to nine months. The students spent about two hours a day listening to and imitating as closely as possible an "informant," that is, a native speaker of the language. Usually the informant was not a professional teacher but merely a native speaker of the language who possessed a good pronunciation. Since the manuals used in the courses provided him with the practice material, his function was simply to pronounce the words and sentences and to make certain that the students imitated him correctly. The description of the structure of the language, to which about three hours a week were devoted, was given by a member of the faculty or by a linguistic specialist invited to participate in the program. This system had several advantages. The amount of time devoted to grammar was limited; and if the linguistic specialist did not pronounce the foreign language too well, he did not influence the students' pronunciation, since they spent more time with the native informant.

Another important feature of the Army method was the extensive use of phonograph records. There were series of records in each of the languages taught, and each student was able to listen to the records again and again until he had perfected his pronunciation.

The Army language course was very intensive. The student spent about 27 hours a week studying the language. Of the 27 hours, about 15 were devoted to drill with the "informant," and about 12 to lectures on the structure of the language and on the history and culture of the nation whose language was being studied. In some cases the students spent even more time on their language studies, yet few students felt that the program was too difficult; the rapid progress they were able to make seemed adequate compensation for their efforts.

Another important feature of the program was the limited size of the classes. Most of them consisted of from 7 to 10 students. The students themselves were very carefully selected.

They had to be over 22 years old, have an IQ of 115 or higher, and show evidence of linguistic aptitude.[29] The language manuals used had a vocabulary range of about 2000 words. Though the words were not taken from frequency lists or lists of basic words, they were selected because of their usefulness. After the first stage in which the student listened to the informant and imitated his pronunciation, the language manuals were used to furnish additional conversational material and to provide selections for reading practice.

Evaluation of the Army Language Program

The Army language program was able to train thousands of soldiers to understand and speak foreign languages in a surprisingly short period of time.[30] The secret of its success is not so much the method employed as the favorable conditions under which the method was carried out. The number of instructional hours per week was five or more times as many as is customary in schools.[31] The groups were carefully selected as to intelligence and linguistic aptitude and limited in numbers, so that each student had ample opportunity to practice the language in class.[32] It is not at all surprising that under these ideal conditions the students made excellent progress.

The important question is whether such a program can be carried out under peacetime conditions. Some of the problems which would have to be solved are:

How can such a program be financed? The sums required would be difficult to obtain even in the largest universities.

Where could we find adult students who would be able to devote six to nine months to language study, not only without financial worries but also with the important incentives (promotion, etc.) offered to the Army students?

It would be difficult indeed to duplicate the conditions of the Army program. There are a number of lessons, however, which we can learn from the program and which we can apply to our present programs:

1) We must begin with the spoken language. Such an approach is not only sounder from the standpoint of the psychology of language learning but makes the work more interesting. Needless to say, only if the student finds the work interesting and profitable is he likely to want to continue.

2) We must re-examine our present curriculum with its separate subjects which are rarely fewer than six a week and

sometimes as high as twelve. It would be better to concentrate
for a certain period of time on one subject and then go on to the
next. It certainly seems to be true that intensive study brings
the highest dividends in the case of language learning.

3) When students begin a foreign language they should study
the pronunciation in small groups. When they begin reading,
it is again possible to have the ordinary class size. Dividing the
class into small groups involves additional expense but it is less
expensive in the long run than wasting the students' time in
classes which are too large for effective language study.

The Desirability of Combining Language and Area Studies

The Army Language Program devoted a great deal of attention to the culture of the nation whose language was being
studied. This was not a complete innovation, for there had
been a tendency in this direction during the last twenty years.[33]
Even earlier there had been a similar trend in the study of the
classical languages. However, relatively little time was spent
on the study of Greek and Latin "realia," and their presentation
usually proved uninspiring. The various language methods
which developed during the last 50 years neglected the cultural
background completely or almost so. Experiments conducted
among American students showed that even those who had
studied French for several years, knew very little about the
political system, literature or art of France. In fact they knew
very little more than those who had never studied French at
all.[33] In the Army program about twelve hours a week were
devoted to "area studies." [34] The teachers in the Army program
discovered, as had many others, that studying the history,
geography, sociology, literature and art of a nation gave the
study of the foreign language more meaning and created in the
student a greater desire to master the language. The area studies
also served to broaden the student's outlook by acquainting him
with societies and cultures quite different in character from
his own. Moreover these studies helped to make the lessons
more interesting—a not unimportant factor; for language study,
no matter how excellent the method used, tends to become tire-
some at times. All modern methods, for example, make use
of songs. The songs may contain words not on the frequency list
but they are important because they give the student some insight into the foreign culture being studied and they help to
enliven the lesson. Many recent language textbooks, including

the Hebrew ones, include folk songs. The reading selections presented in the text should also have a cultural background. The cultural material ought not to be relegated to the appendix but should form part of the text. It is naturally not easy to prepare material of this sort within the limited vocabulary of the beginner, but many textbook writers have achieved a considerable measure of success. Where the teacher finds it impossible to lecture on the cultural background in the foreign language, it is better to use the student's native language than to forego such lectures entirely.

The Intensive Hebrew Course in Israel—"Ulpan"

The Ministry of Education and Culture in Israel and the Immigration Department of the Jewish Agency set up a number of courses for the intensive study of Hebrew. An experimental course was established in Jerusalem and proved so successful that similar courses were opened in other centers where there were large groups of newcomers.

Though the teachers in these intensive courses were all experienced in language teaching, they had had no experience with adult courses, and in some respects they had to work out their program as they went along. On the basis of the first course held at the immigrant camp "Etzion" in Jerusalem, it is possible to give a provisional evaluation of the work.

The experiment was primarily intended for recent immigrants who have adequate cultural and professional experience but are unable to find their place in the new environment because of ignorance of Hebrew. These were enabled to live and to study in the "ulpan" (resident college, studio) for about half a year.

The courses required large expenditures. The Department of Education took care of the teachers' salaries, equipment, books, etc., and the Immigration Department of the Jewish Agency met the expenses involved in housing and maintaining the students. The students undertook to return part of these expenditures when they had finally learned enough Hebrew to find positions. In order to reduce expenses and to take care of the growing number of students, intensive courses were opened in various rural settlements. Young students were sent to these centers for six months and studied half a day and worked the rest, using their earnings to help cover the cost of the courses.

During the first term of the Jerusalem course there were about 25 students in a class. The average age was 45, though there were some as old as 65. The classes were made as homogeneous as possible. The students studied 6 hours a day—3 in the morning and 3 in the afternoon. Each teacher worked out his own program. Textbooks were used to some extent, but since there are few which are at once easy and interesting it was necessary to make extensive use of newspapers and magazines. In order to create a group spirit there were frequent parties and singing sessions, and in order to acquaint the students with the country there were talks and lectures, trips to historical sites, exhibitions, museums, etc.

The students who participated in the first course came from 25 countries and spoke almost as many languages. This was an advantage in a way since Hebrew became the common denominator for them all. Among the students there were some who knew a little Hebrew and others who did not even know the alphabet. The classes were divided, therefore, into beginners and advanced. By the time the course ended the students in the advanced classes had perfected their Hebrew and the beginners were able to converse freely in Hebrew and to read unvocalized texts.

The success of the course was due to its intensive character and to the enthusiasm of the teachers. Many of the students who completed the course were immediately able to secure positions in their professions. The language courses can accordingly become an important factor in the economic absorption of the immigrants.

The Importance of Establishing Linguistic Ties Between Israel and the Diaspora

It is difficult to come to know the culture of Israel unless one can come into direct contact with it. One means of setting up linguistic ties between Israel and the Diaspora is through Pen Clubs. "Ha-Keren Ha-Kayemet" and other institutions and organizations have already taken the first steps. The practice of having students exchange letters is widespread in other countries.[35] The League of Nations sponsored such a program, and the United Nations is now undertaking a similar program involving thousands of students. Pen Clubs are important in fostering ties between Israel and the Diaspora, and more energetic efforts than have hitherto been made are now necessary. Another important means of bringing the culture of any "foreign" country closer to students is to have them spend a certain period of time (the summer vacation usually) in the home of a family in that country.[36] One good means of achieving this is through the granting of scholarships. Scholarships would enable hundreds and thousands of students in the Diaspora to come to the Hebrew University and other educational institutions in Israel for an extended period of time. No better means could be found of spreading Hebrew culture in the Diaspora.

But our task is also to encourage the study of Hebrew outside Israel. In this respect we should not restrict our efforts to Hebrew schools and classes. We need to set up circles [37] to which young people can come not only to study Hebrew and to take courses in Hebrew literature and art, but also to participate in group singing and dancing and in plays, to listen to Hebrew records and broadcasts, and to watch Hebrew films. An interesting institution in Israel along these lines is the "Bet Tarbut" ("Home of Culture"). These "Homes of Culture" which have been established in various centers serve for both recreational and cultural purposes. Here an immigrant can not only take the Hebrew courses but listen to the Hebrew spoken around him. A somewhat similar function is performed by the Hebrew summer camps in the U. S. where youngsters have an opportunity to hear and speak Hebrew all day during the vacation months.

The Use of Audio-Visual Aids

It is scarcely necessary today to emphasize the importance of audio-visual aids in the teaching of languages. The value of phonograph records has generally been recognized,[38] and more and more schools are making use of them both as a means of enabling students to learn the sounds of the foreign language and to make it possible for them to hear the foreign language spoken by natives when they might not otherwise have the opportunity. Many American schools set aside a number of "laboratory periods" during which students listen to records time and again until they are able to follow them without difficulty or, in the latter stages, to reproduce what they have heard. Wire or tape recorders are also very useful for this purpose. They are particularly helpful in enabling students to correct pronunciation mistakes, for many students are unaware of their own mispronunciations until they actually hear them.

Listening to radio broadcasts can be very valuable. The Hebrew broadcasts from Jerusalem, London and New York should be used for instructional purposes with advanced students. It is not advisable, though, to introduce radio broadcasts in a foreign language too early, lest the students become discouraged, before they start, by a jumble of unfamiliar sounds that may induce in the initial stages of training a "language terror" [39] effect. Films and television are of very great importance, since they combine auditory and visual impressions. The language teaching films produced so far have on the whole not been very successful.[39] For the most part their vocabulary load is too great and the material itself not too interesting. Another serious fault is that the films are not integrated into the course of study.[40] Still, there can be little doubt as to the effectiveness of properly prepared films. They can be an effective means of spreading the knowledge of Hebrew in the Diaspora, and it is to be hoped that the various Israeli governmental and semi-governmental agencies which are concerned with this problem will consider the preparation of suitable films. Far less costly than films are filmstrips accompanied by records, a combination which produces a lasting bond between the visual and the acoustic impressions of the learner. This audio-visual medium seems to hold out a great promise in the field of language training in Hebrew.

Extensive use should also be made of other visual devices such as flash cards, drawings, photographs, stereopticon slides,[41] vocabulary films,[42] dioramas, etc. Nor must we overlook the use of dramatization. Full-dress plays require considerable expenditures for costumes and scenery and can therefore at best be presented only once or twice a year. But much the same results can be achieved by having the students act out situations, dramatize stories, personify fables, etc.[43]

Some promising experiments have also been made with the techniques of psycho-drama or socio-drama.[44] The student is given several minutes during which he says whatever comes to mind and no attempt is made to correct his mistakes. In this way the students are often able to break down any inhibitions they may have about speaking a foreign language and gradually develop self-confidence in its use. Such psycho-drama technique can be employed with success in immigrants' camps, "Homes of Culture," in Hebrew "circles" and summer camps.

NOTES TO CHAPTER FIVE

1. In his speech in honor of Wieland (Febr. 18, 1813).

2. Compare the Italian proverb: *Traduttore traditore.*

3. Jespersen, Otto, *How to Teach a Foreign Language* (1944), p. 82.

4. Palmer, H. E. and Redman, H. V., *This Language Learning Business* (1932), p. 198.

5. Jespersen, *op. cit.*, p. 57.

6. This view is opposed by C. T. Buswell in his *Laboratory Study of the Reading of Modern Foreign Languages* (1927), p. 73ff. His experiments show that the direct method is superior to the translation method in developing reading ability.

7. Angiolillo, P. F., *Armed Forces Foreign Language Teaching* (1947), p. 109ff.

8. Palmer, H. E., *Colloquial English I,* 100 *Substitution Tables* (1942), p. XIIff.

9. Jespersen, *op. cit.*, p. 58.

10. Handschin, *op. cit.*, p. 71.

11. Kaulfers, H. V., *Modern Languages for Modern Schools* (1942), p. 101f.

12. *Encyclopedia of Modern Education* (1950), p. 534.

13. *Ibid.*, p. 660.

14. Handschin, *op. cit.*, p. 71.

15. Bloomfield, L., *op. cit.*, p. 503.

16. The Berlitz Method is based on the following principles: 1) Practice in speaking precedes practice in writing; 2) Reading and writing are taught after the student has learned to speak; 3) In the class-drills the teacher asks a question and the student replies with a full sentence; 4) Progress is achieved only through the active participation of the pupil; 5) The student's own language is not used (as a result there is no translation work of any kind; 6) Grammar is studied only in the later stages and then only in the form of examples; 7) All language instruction has a practical orientation and therefore the material is drawn from life.

17. Handschin, *op cit.*, p. 66.

18. Lind, *op. cit.*, p. 14f.

19. Schlüter, L., *Zeitschrift für Psychologie* (1914).

20. Shaltkowska, G., *Zeitschrift für Angewandte Psychologie,* v. 25 (1925), p. 65ff.

21. Agard, F. B. and Dunkel, H. B., *An Investigation of Second*

Language Teaching (1948), p. 19ff.

22. Jespersen, *op. cit.*, p. 84.

23. Palmer, *op. cit.*, p. VI.

24. *Ibid.*, p. 6.

25. Bloomfield, *op. cit.*, p. 21.

26. Fries, *op. cit.*, p. 6ff.

27. Bradley, Henry, *"On the Relations between Spoken and Written Language,"* Proceedings of the Britsh Academy, v. VI, p. 17f.

28. Agard and Dunkel, *op. cit.*, p. 181ff.

29. Lind, *op. cit.*, p. 117.

30. A very full description of the Army Language Program (ASTP) can be found in Angiolillo's book mentioned above.

31. Lind, *op. cit.*, p. 27.

32. Michael West computed the time that a student in the average language class has for the active use of the language. He found that in a class of 30 which lasts for 45 minutes and in which the teacher speaks half the period, each student has less than 1 minute for recitation.

33. *Encyclopedia of Modern Education,* p. 535.

34. Angiolillo, *op. cit.*, pp. 138-142.

35. Cole and Tharp, *op. cit.*, p. 251ff.

36. This is quite common practice in Europe. See Handschin, *op. cit.*, p. 303.

37. Similar to Le Cercle Français or the British Council. See Cole and Tharp, *op. cit.*, pp. 227-230.

38. Agard and Dunkel, *op. cit.*, p. 286.

39. Duff, *op. cit.*, p. 62ff.

40. Angiolillo, *op. cit.*, p. 116.

41. For details, see *Teachers Manual, A Guide for Teaching English to the Foreign Born* (Committee for Refugee Education, New York, 1949), p. 7ff.

42. Gelman, M., "Some General Ideas on Visual Aids in Modern Language Teaching," *Visual Aids Review,* v. 1 (Melbourne University Press, 1950), p. 25f.

43. For these impromtu dramatizations (called "comédie spontanée"), see Angiolillo, *op. cit.*, p. 90ff.

44. Moreno, J. L., *Psychodrama* (1946).

CHAPTER SIX

THE PRINCIPLES OF THE JERUSALEM METHOD

"Dynamic Eclecticism"

The fundamental problem in pedagogy is not which particular method is the best, but rather when to use one method and when to use another. We have yet to discover a universal method which would be the best for all types of students, at all levels, and no matter what one's objectives may be. To think in terms of such a panacea is naive.

Only an eclectic approach—one which selects from various methods what is best suited to the age of the learner, his IQ, his stage of progress and his purpose in learning a foreign language —can take full advantage of the advances in educational theory and experimentation. It is of course true that in the field of language-teaching a number of important matters still need to be established experimentally, if indeed they ever can be, since in many cases individual differences play so important a role. Yet enough has been achieved to assure us of a reasonable measure of success in language teaching—a greater measure certainly than if we adopt a dogmatic or a monistic approach. Even methods which have not generally proved successful, such as for example those based on formal grammar or mechanical drill, can in certain special cases be used with profit. Thus, an advanced student with a talent for languages may enjoy and benefit from the study of formal grammar, while a student with a low IQ and with little language aptitude may profit most from frequent drills.

On the other hand, even the best methods must be used at the proper time and in the proper place. The direct method is more suitable for younger students, while the translation method usually proves most satisfactory with older students or with very bright ones. The aural-oral method is excellent indeed; and yet if the student happens to be a scientist interested in deciphering ancient texts, it is clearly inadvisable to use this method extensively. Many students find the aural-conversational method interesting in the first stages but are likely to grow bored unless interesting reading selections are soon introduced. Developing the ability to understand the spoken language and to speak the language does not automatically result in an ability to read it, as many language teachers believed. To learn to read a language requires specific drill, preferably given after the student has learned to understand the spoken language and to speak it to some degree. Developing an ability to understand and speak is one problem; learning to read is quite another. Each skill requires specific drill and method; and though there is some transfer from one skill to another, it is relatively small.[1] For this reason the eclectic approach employs different methods depending on the circumstances—the student's purpose in learning the language, his age, his ability, and other factors.

But the eclectic approach, however adroitly managed, is not in itself the solution to the language teaching problem. The right selection of method is essential for success, but no less crucial than the selection of the teaching devices is their dynamic execution. A dynamic set-up is necessary for the proper functioning of an activity, and particularly for the initial phases. The best teaching technique cannot replace the force of motivation. We have been cautioned time and again against drawing general conclusions from the widely used laboratory method of experimentation with nonsense syllables [2] in the studies of learning. There is a world of difference between the study of nonsense syllables and the study of meaningful material. It is possible, indeed, that a student who finds it very difficult to remember simple nonsense syllables may have little difficulty in remembering complex material that has particular meaning for him. Motivating conditions occupy the center of the stage of learning and have a special bearing on the effectiveness of memorization and repetition.

Repetition Alone Brings No Improvement

The importance of repetition in the learning process has long been recognized but has also been overemphasized. The Hebrew saying "One who has studied his lesson a hundred times cannot be compared to one who has studied it a hundred and one times" illustrates the importance attached in Jewish tradition to the constant repetition of material to be learned. Similarly, we find numerous proverbs or adages in Greek, Roman and European languages expressing the idea that frequent repetition is the source of all knowledge. This quantitative approach to the learning process was proposed as a scientific theory by followers of Watson and his Behavioristic School, and by followers of Pavlov and his theory of the conditioned reflex. According to this school of thought, learning depends on the intensity of stimuli and reactions within the nervous system. If the stimuli are sufficiently numerous and recent, then a bond becomes established and learning takes place. On the other hand, if the stimuli or reactions are decreased in number or if they are not constantly repeated, the bond becomes weaker and the material learned is forgotten. This quantitative conception of learning is now considered oversimplified, to say the least. We are coming to appreciate more and more that learning is a very complex matter and that the laws of remembering and forgetting are still imperfectly understood.[3] The mechanistic explanation of learning as a strengthening of neural bonds was merely a hypothesis and has never been proved. Human learning cannot be conceived of as merely a sum of simple learning processes as discharged by human beings against the artificial background of a laboratory. Many human learning processes are incomparably more complicated, and language learning is a good example.

It is accordingly difficult to agree with those language teachers who hold that success in language learning depends entirely or mainly on the number of times items are repeated and the frequency with which they are drilled. There is no question that learning involves frequent repetition and drill, but there is no direct correlation between progress in learning and the number of repetitions. The mere fact that an item is repeated does not ensure retention. Very frequently a saturation point is reached and further repetitions have no effect, or an adverse effect.[4] Learning depends on certain psychological factors—interest, motivation, concentration, striving toward a goal, etc. Repetition affords opportunity for exhibiting these psychological elements and, insofar as they are brought into play, learning takes place or improves. But unless the psychological factors are present the mere repetition of an item will have no effect, just as (to quote the illustration used by a noted psychologist) a wire may transmit a message thousands of times and yet no effect is left on the wire itself. Repetition or practice is no guarantee of learning if the proper psychological "set" is absent;[5] and only if it is present and only to the degree in which it is present will repetition or practice have a positive effect.

Related and Meaningful Material—the Vital Factor

We have already had occasion to emphasize that adults make more rapid progress in language learning than children or even adolescents (except in the acquisition of speaking habits). Of the four factors which, according to Thorndike, determine success in learning, namely, health and energy, ability to learn, interest, and opportunities for learning, adults excel as regards interest, and this fact alone gives them a great advantage. Interest and the desire to learn are more decisive than any other factors in determining success in learning. The studies in remembering carried out by Mrs. Zeigarnik[6] are very instructive in this respect. She experimented with finished and unfinished tasks, with tasks which were interrupted and with those which were brought to a conclusion. Her experiments showed that recall was best for incompleted and interrupted tasks.[7] The explanation is to be found in the fact that when a task was completed mental "tension"[8] was relaxed. This tension or urge is the most important factor in learning. A child learns his mother tongue rapidly because of it. "The child has an inherent natural urge to learn to communicate with its mother or nurse," and this urge "is the most important thing to have in setting about learning a foreign language." We must "consider its absence as one of the most important reasons why boys and girls at school make poor progress in their linguistic studies."[9]

The essential problem in language teaching is how to create the proper psychological "tension" in the student studying the foreign language. To a very great extent it is dependent upon the quality of the material presented and the manner in which it is organized. "From a rapidly growing volume of research . . . the outlines of a constructive view of learning, sharply set off from practices which relied on formal drill, are taking form. This point of view emphasizes relatedness rather than itemization."[10]

The material should be presented not as a conglomeration of separate and unrelated items but as an organized whole. Only in this way can the learning process be made meaningful and thus efficient. The student receives an overall view of the material and can consequently see the relation of each item to the whole. He is taught to approach the parts as disengaged from the whole, and not to treat the whole as an assemblage of fragments.

A good example of this principle can be found in the studies of word frequency which have been carried out in the last two generations and which represent one of the most significant recent advances in the field of pedagogy. An objective procedure was worked out for determining word frequencies and a detailed analysis was made of the vocabulary of a number of languages. But merely determining which words are most frequent does not solve our problem. It is useless to present each word as a separate item. The most frequent words have to be presented in the form of interesting learning units and the knowledge of the individual words must come as a by-product. The memorization of isolated words is one of the worst evils in language teaching—Bacon indeed calls it the very worst ("omnium molestissima"). Studying words in isolation is unsound not only psychologically but also semantically. In many cases it is impossible to say what a word means until we know the context. The exact meaning of a word cannot be given in advance; one can only give an approximate indication of the general semantic field it covers. "All words within a given context interact upon one another" [11]; and only when the word occurs in a particular context can a definite meaning be given for it. The starting point in language teaching is the thought unit, and only when that is made the basis of instruction can students make rapid progress.

Nor is the use of sentences of the type: "What did you have for breakfast?" or "How did you spend the summer?" a marked improvement over the use of isolated words.[12] Topics like these serve as poor motivation and can hardly gain the interest of an intelligent student. Only significant themes and instructional material based on related and coherent wholes can sustain the learning process on a high level.

Related and meaningful material served as the basis of the "Jerusalem Method" which has been worked out by the author in Jerusalem for mature and adolescent students. The first book incorporating this method is to appear shortly.[13] It is intended for English-speaking beginners who know the Hebrew alphabet, and provides material for the first 80-100 hours of instruction.

The Essential Feature of the Jerusalem Method—
Unified and Meaningful Material

The primary aim of the Jerusalem method is to create the proper psychological "tension" in the students. The dynamic organization of the instructional material is designed to arouse the interest of the students from the very start. The reading matter is presented in the form of a narrative portraying life and experiences in modern Israel. Conversations and discussions are expanded on certain incidents in the story with the result that the entire reading matter of the text, in spite of its variety, is organically related and gives the impression of a unified whole.

In order to vary the material, songs are introduced in each unit. Even these songs fit into the general scheme since they are selected according to their content and vocabulary and are introduced in their appropriate places. Anecdotes to enliven the text are included occasionally and in small doses, since instructional material that consists largely of humorous anecdotes and jokes is as likely as not to annoy most students.[14] This, however, is not true of songs, provided that they are chosen with due regard to their themes and vocabulary load.[15] Songs (particularly if accompanied by the musical notation) appeal to all ages, and they can do much to create an emotional attachment to the language and culture.

The essence of the Jerusalem Method is thus variety within unity—varied material forming part of a unified meaningful whole.

Lexical and Grammatical Elements Must
Be Carefully Chosen

All of the Hebrew text, even in the first book for beginners, is written in Hebrew characters and in the conventional spelling. In the first ten units of the first book (representing together 30 to 40 hours of instruction) all the Hebrew is also given in transcription as a help to the beginner, but the transcription is dropped very early. Experience has shown that most students prefer to study a language in the conventional writing system rather than in phonetic transcription.[16]

In order to fulfill these conditions and to have enough of a dramatic story element to hold the students' interest, existing stories cannot be used, since they are written for people whose mother tongue is Hebrew and therefore use a vocabulary entirely out of the range of the beginner. Even those parts of the Bible which are written in a simple style are too difficult for the beginner. Material for beginners must be written within a very limited vocabulary range, and words must be constantly repeated. New words should be introduced only after the other words have been learned. Even after the first lessons the proportion of new words to old should be something like 1 to 50.[17]

In the Jerusalem Method great care is taken to use only the most frequent and basic words. Each word is repeated at least five times, which is usually considered sufficient; [18] but most of the vocabulary is repeated many times with due consideration to the effect of "overlearning" on retention.

Anyone who has ever tried to create interesting reading and conversational matter within the limits so narrowly defined by lexical and grammatical considerations realizes the difficulty of the task. Since it calls for the literary talents of the professional author and the pedagogical knowledge and experience of a teacher, it generally requires a team of an author and teacher, except in cases where one person happens to be both. After the first hundred hours of instruction—that is, after the students have completed the beginning text—it is desirable to introduce them to selections from literature. In Hebrew many of the biblical stories should be used—the stories of Jacob, Joseph, Moses, Samuel, Saul, David, Solomon, Jeremiah, Job, Ruth, Jonah, and others. One can also use selections from medieval and modern literature but the vocabulary must be simplified for beginning students.

Bilingual Texts and Illustrations

Bilingual Hebrew texts [19] with graded reading material have been used with considerable success.[20]

It is best to give the original text and the translation on facing pages.[21] It is not desirable to give the translation after every line, section or chapter, or at the end of the book, because the student loses the continuity, or else has to leaf back and forth. Moreover, in the case of Hebrew it is confusing to give an interlinear translation since Hebrew is read from left to right.

When bilingual texts are used it is important that the student should read the original paragraph by paragraph, or chapter by chapter, without consulting the translation. He should try to determine the meaning of new words or idioms from the context, and only after he has finished the entire paragraph or chapter should he read the translation to see whether he has understood the passage correctly. As the student progresses the amount of material translated can be reduced. Eventually he can be furnished with a translation of only those portions that are likely to prove difficult.

After the beginning text has been completed, or even in conjunction with it, it is well to use drawings and photographs to familiarize the student with the Jewish milieu in Israel and in the Diaspora. There should be a commentary in simple Hebrew with an explanation of the difficult words. The student should be introduced as early as possible to easy selections from newspapers and magazines. The literary quality of such selections may not always be of the highest order; but on the other hand the material is of interest because it "deals with realities, with 'situations' in the contemporary world" [22] and is of value in that it helps build up the "cultural background" of the student.

The Sentence As the Basic Unit

The Jerusalem Method uses the sentence as the basic unit. The sentences are kept as simple as possible in the first lessons and are gradually made longer and more complicated in structure. One of the most important features of the Jerusalem Method is that the learner becomes accustomed from the very start to material in connected discourse. If a student studies words in isolation he may reach a point where he is able to understand every word in the sentence and yet not grasp the meaning of the sentence as a whole. The normal unit of expression is the thought unit, and the order in which the text should be assimilated is therefore: units of thought—sentences —words.[23] The complete unit is first presented to the student, and only after he has learned it as a whole does he begin to analyze it into its component parts. Lexical and grammatical analysis should take place within the framework of the sentence so that the student can from the outset learn to form sentences. The material should be easy enough in the beginning for the student to be able to grasp it, but it should not be made so very easy that the student feels no challenge. This well-known principle has been confirmed by experiments even in animal learning.[24]

Another feature of the Jerusalem Method is the testing program. All students, whether young or mature, need to be able to check their progress by means of self-administered tests or tests administered by the teacher. The Jerusalem Method tests the student's comprehension of material presented in the form of complete sentences. The student is given correct and incorrect sentences and asked to choose the correct ones, thus revealing whether he has understood them. The other types of examination used are also based upon the same principle, so that the sentences serve not only as a test but at the same time as additional practice material.

A Synthesis of Aural-Oral Approach and Modified Translation

The Jerusalem Method is eclectic in the sense that it is based both on aural-conversational approach, and on what in the preceding chapter was termed "modified translation." The translation is given facing the original and it decreases in amount as the student progresses. Translation is always from the Hebrew to the student's mother tongue, and whole sentences are translated, not isolated words alone. This synthesis of the two methods vitalizes the initial phases of language learning, broadens its scope, and helps the student to learn to read in as short a period of time as possible.[25]

Other essential features of the Jerusalem Method are imitation and practice of complete sentences and connected passages. Particular attention is paid to correct pronunciation. The student is asked to imitate as accurately as he can the pronunciation of his teacher or that which he hears on the phonograph records accompanying the text. The pronunciation taught is the Sephardic pronunciation as spoken in Israel today.

In the first phases the process is mechanical; the student listens to sentences pronounced by his teacher or spoken on the records, and repeats them until he knows them by heart. In the next stage the average student begins to analyze the material and to acquire a knowledge of the grammatical structure of the language. The text of the narrative and the conversations are used for purposes of grammatical analysis,[26] and the grammatical features are arrived at inductively. Similarities and differences between Hebrew and English vocabulary, grammar and idiomatic usage are constantly pointed out. Special attention is paid to prepositions, pronouns, adverbs, and to the so-called "small words" which are so important in most languages and particularly so in an analytic language like Hebrew.

One of the prominent features of the Jerusalem Method is

its attempt to apply faithfully the important advances made during the last fifty years in the field of vocabulary analysis (see Chapter Four). About 90 per cent of the vocabulary presented during the first 80-100 hours of instruction is taken from the list of the most frequent words and from the list of basic words. A deliberate effort is made to effect an active "transfer" into Hebrew from "cognate" expressions used in Yiddish or in current Jewish or Israeli usage.

The Jerusalem Method also makes extensive use of "realia" and includes material on the customs, ideals and experiences of the Jewish people, the Zionist movement, the geography of Israel, and life in Israel today. This material is presented not only in English but is interwoven into the Hebrew text.

1. Agard and Dunkel, *op. cit.*, p. 158, 291ff.

2. Dunkel, H. B., *Second-Language Learning* (1948), p. 167, and Hilgard, E. R., *Theories of Learning* (1948), p. 222.

3. *Encyclopedia of Educational Research* (1941), p. 674.

4. Hilgard, *op. cit.*, p. 218. "Too much repetition does not aid learning; on the contrary, repetition may lead to psychological satiation with accompanying disorganization. . . . With better arrangements fewer repetitions are needed. This is the lesson of the insight experiments."

5. See Thomson, G. H., *Instinct, Intelligence and Character* (1924).

6. Zeigarnik, B., "Das Behalten erledigter und unerledigter Handlungen," *Psych. Forsch.,* IX (1927), pp. 1-85.

7. Hilgard, *op .cit.,* p. 226ff.

8. For the terms "tension" and "tension-system," see Hilgard, *op. cit.,* p. 226.

9. Duff, *op. cit.,* p. 12f.

10. Gates, I. G. *et al., Educational Psychology* (1942), p. 344.

11. Hayakawa, S. J., *Language in Action* (1947), p. 49ff.

12. Lind, *op. cit.,* p. 62ff.

13. Rieger, E. (in collaboration with Indelman, E.), *Everyday Hebrew,* Youth Department of the Jewish Agency, Jerusalem (1953).

14. Jespersen, O., *How to Teach a Foreign Language* (1944), p. 24.

15. Cole and Tharp, *op. cit.,* p. 236ff.

16. Dunkel, *op. cit.,* p. 98.

17. Russell, H. J., "What is Readable and What is not Readable in a Foreign Language," *Modern Language Journal* (April, 1950), p. 275.

18. Dunkel, *op. cit.,* p. 152.

19. Bilingual Hebrew and English texts have been issued in the United States by H. A. Friedland and by Solomon Goldman.

20. The Toussaint-Langenscheidt Method used literary selections as reading material. The method was successful from the point of view of content; but since no attempt was made to grade the lexical and grammatical material according to difficulty and introduce it by stages, most students found the method impossibly difficult (see Chapter Five).

21. The assumption is that the student will not read the translation until he has finished reading the original, but this does not usually hold true with young students who are apt to consult the translation when they do not know a word or indeed to read the whole translation through if it is interesting. However, this method works well with adult students and with the more serious adolescent students.

22. Duff, *op. cit.*, p. 72.

23. Angiolillo, *op .cit.*, p. 18, 79.

24. *Encyclopedia of Educational Research, op. cit.*, p. 738.

25. Dunkel, *op. cit.*, p. 194.

26. Angiolillo, *op. cit., p.* 132f.